DATE DUE

DEMCO 38-296

Tiny

Tiny Houses

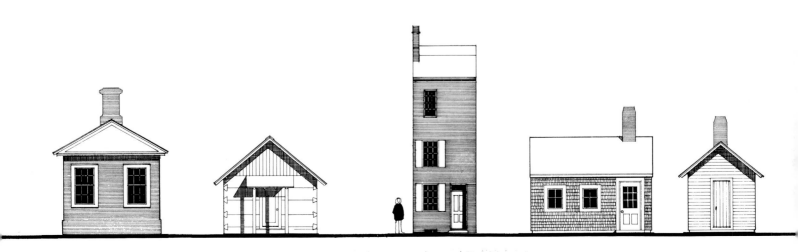

Tiny

Tiny Houses

Lester Walker

The Overlook Press
Woodstock, New York

Woodstock, New York 12498

Library of Congress Cataloging-in-Publication Data

Walker, Les.
Tiny houses.

1. Small houses — United States — Designs and plans —
Amateurs' manuals. 2. Architecture, Domestic — United States
— Designs and Plans — Amateurs' manuals. I. Title.
NA7205.W36 1987   728.3'7'0222   86-21736
ISBN 0-87951-271-7

Jacket photographs by Lester Walker except for Poetry House
by William Seitz and Earthquake Refugee Shack by Jim Kanne.

Tenth Printing

Printed in Singapore

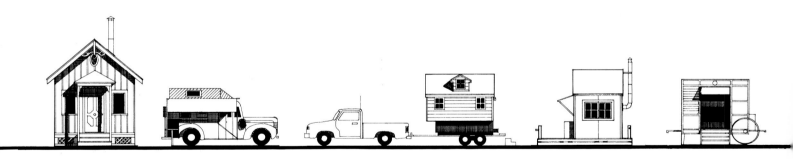

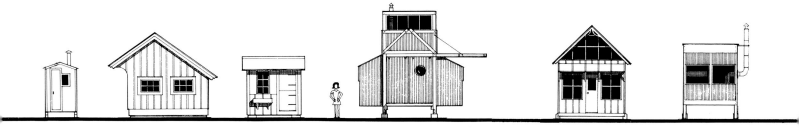

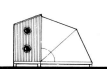

To my wife Karen and my sons Jess and Andrew

Contents

Introduction

This book began four years ago as a pattern book illustrating several tiny houses as affordable build-it-yourself vacation homes. The idea was to provide the reader with plans for very, very inexpensive small dwelling projects that would take a week or two to build. My goal was to inspire people of all ages and degrees of carpentry skill who previously could not afford a second home to take hammer in hand and build themselves a little dream. It seems to me that one of the great thrills in life is to inhabit a building that one has built oneself. *Tiny Houses* was to be the answer for those who wanted this experience.

Ever since the first manned space capsule was sent into orbit in 1961 I have been interested in perfectly designed tiny living spaces. I kept careful notes on projects that I liked and began gathering plans for houses with under three hundred square feet of space that might easily be detailed and described. A few years ago I contacted Michael Jantzen, Jeff Milstein, Allan Wexler, and Mary Carrabba, and they agreed to allow me to include their work. I challenged my City College architecture students to design a tiny house of their own, and some of those were to be included here. The book took shape. I would include about twenty tiny houses with schematic plans showing how they could be constructed. Just when I had collected a nice list of tiny houses and had begun laying out the book, the idea began to change. First, practically every conversation I entered that began with "What are you doing lately?" ended in a discussion of some incredible tiny house that I hadn't considered I particularly remember three years ago in Reston, Virginia, speaking with a group of people who had assembled to celebrate the opening of *House Beautiful* magazine's "Best Small House '84," a national house design competition that I had won. After someone asked me "What's next?" the representative of the American Wood Council, sponsors of the competition, editors of two local newspapers, a *House Beautiful* editor, and a Reston advertising executive and his wife became absorbed in the idea of tiny houses. I learned about Thoreau's cabin, the Martha's Vineyard Campground cottages, and the tiny writer's huts in which Hollywood movie scriptwriters in the 1930s were forced to stay until they completed their jobs. I also learned to bring up the tiny-house subject whenever I could, because it seemed like everyone had a favorite that could take me on a tiny house-hunting adventure.

Second, I found that as I laid out the book I was spending more time and space showing how to build the house than how it looked, how it came to be, or how it felt to be inside. I found that I was borrowing too much from books that explained building methods much better than I could.

I decided then that I could best serve the reader by providing more inspirational information, such as pictures of the buildings, drawings of interior furniture layouts, construction sequences showing how easy it is, and the story of the house. I included the basic architectural drawings of elevations and plans, having concluded that once the reader chose a house, he or she could use these drawings together with a housebuilding guide (listed in the Bibliography) to build his or her tiny house. In short, the book evolved from a builder's guide of about twenty houses to a historical compilation of over forty houses, showing space use and special details such as a key construction method or material use, or a bathroom or kitchen design.

Ideally, *Tiny Houses* will inspire those in need to dream and to build. It will provide a source book showing how tiny tiny houses can be, and it will give architects, historians, builders, preservationists, students, and house lovers over forty interesting, relevant, short stories with which to spend an evening.

Notes about the Houses:

The first tiny house I remember seeing and categorizing as a tiny, tiny house was a complete surprise. In the summer of 1963, I discovered one while hiking along what seemed to me to be a very treacherous untraveled animal trail on a remote part of Maine's coastline, about an hour east of Cutler. I couldn't imagine how anyone might have transported materials to this spot without having lugged them over windswept cliffs and slippery rocks. But there it was, a tiny little gable-roofed cabin no larger than 8' x 10' built entirely of tarpaper and driftwood, complete with an Adirondack style built-in twig bed, a perfect little kitchen that used water from a nearby spring, and a writing desk under a window facing the sea. Set back about one hundred feet from the ocean on a rocky beach in a small cove, the house was surrounded by cliffs topped with huge hemlock and pine trees. Later, when I got back to town and learned that it was built by a little lady in her eighties who loved nature and solitude, I realized that the art of building was not necessarily reserved for architects and builders. All that was needed, it seemed, was the will. Two years ago, I hiked back to this site with my camera, notepad, and the hope that I could find this little building to include in *Tiny Houses*. No luck. A big storm had apparently blown it away. But this home will remain in my mind as one of the most beautiful buildings I've ever seen. It may well have been the inspiration for this book.

My early research was done primarily by mail or phone. For example, one day a photograph of a tiny house appeared in my mail accompanied by a letter from my aunt and uncle who had just visited the Carmel Bay area in California and had photographed one of many tiny houses in a community there. When

I asked them where it was they could only provide me with the name of the motel where they had stayed. I wrote to the motel and asked them to slip a letter under the door of the tiny house, enclosing the photograph so the motel might find it. Miraculously, I received a return letter from the owners of the Pink House including a bit of history and some sketched floor plans. My detective work had paid off. The house is included in the book along with my uncle's photograph.

Later, as I began to need more information about the houses, I planned visits to draw and discuss them in person. One of my more recent tiny house-hunting adventures happened last winter on a quest to photograph ice fishing shanties in Upstate New York. As I walked over the slick twenty-four-inch-thick ice of Lake Champlain I had no idea how far I was from shore: my mind was focused on the wonderful little communities of buildings—each one more exciting than the last. When I realized that it was snowing and the wind was beginning to howl, I looked for my car on shore. I couldn't see it. To add to my anxiety, I learned that I had to shuffle my feet because the fresh layer of snow made the ice much more slippery. By the time I got to my car, about two miles later, I was caked with snow, my legs were rubbery with exhaustion, and my nose was frozen. I felt like Admiral Perry in the Arctic, tracking the elusive ice fishing shanty.

Another adventure—to photograph dune shacks—took me across the great sand dunes at the tip of Cape Cod near Provincetown. I missed my contact, a ten-year-old daughter of a friend of a friend, who was to escort me to the shacks. Because my time was limited I decided to make the trip myself. I had no idea it was like the Sahara out there! My destination was only about a forty-minute walk away but the heat off the sand, the difficulty in walking, and the desolate dune landscape drained my energy and made me quite thirsty, to say the least. Luckily, a cool glass of water and a friendly face greeted me before too long in the shack known as Thalasa.

Researching this book has been a wonderful experience. Almost every house seemed to begin with an idea from a book, magazine, friend, or colleague; lead to a most interesting, sometimes thrilling photography/sketching/interview session; and end with a quiet week at my graphics table synthesizing my information into drawings and pasting up camera-ready mechanical boards from which this book was printed.

I am sure most people, if they so desired, could research their own list of tiny houses just as remarkable as those illustrated here. If I had written this book at a different time in my life, the houses would probably have been entirely different. Once one starts seriously observing and studying, the number of tiny houses in any given geographical area can be endless.

Notes on Building:

There are no plans available for any of the tiny houses shown in this book. Please do not send letters asking for plans. If you choose to build one of the houses, the basic dimensions, materials, and methods are discussed, but a complete set of construction drawings was impossible to include. If you are a beginning builder, it is suggested that you read one or two of the basic housebuilding books listed in the Bibliography and then become very friendly with a local housebuilder. If you have housebuilding experience, the information given should be adequate. It is my intention to inspire you to participate in the design and construction of your home, making it fit your needs and site; learn about the art of building; and after you've completed your structure, experience the excitement of living in the house that you built.

Notes on the Photographs:

All of the photographs in the book are by me except those listed on page 220. These people were kind enough to share their work with me. A few photographs in the book are snapshots of demolished houses or photographs that I could not reproduce. I apologize for their poor quality but I felt that the houses they depicted were worthy of inclusion.

Notes about the Drawings:

All of the drawings were done on 100 percent rag tracing paper at ⅛" = 1'0" scale with 4x0 and 2x0 Mars Staetler ink pens. They were reduced with photostats to 68 percent of their original size for the final graphics of the book. Because all the drawings are drawn to the same scale, they can be compared to one another throughout the book. The patterns were drawn at ¹⁄₁₆" = 1'0" scale and also reduced 68 percent. They are designed to be copied and cut out and folded so that each tiny house shape can be fully appreciated.

Finally, I'd like to express what a great experience every aspect of this book was, from research to final artwork and editing. I have many new friends because of it and a fresh outlook on my architecture and teaching. I hope this appreciation comes through, and I do hope you enjoy the book.

Lester Walker
Woodstock, New York

Tiny Historic Houses

Recreated Plymouth Colony, Plymouth, Massachusetts

English Settlers' Cottage

14' x 12' plus sleeping loft
168 square feet

Among America's first houses were tiny houses. In the early 1620s, the English settlers, particularly in New England and Virginia, built their homes using methods imported from medieval England: thick post-and-beam frame, thin wall studs and roof rafters, wooden twigs attached to the studs and covered with mud for insulation, a steep thatched grass roof, hand-split oak clapboards, and an 8-foot-wide stone fireplace.

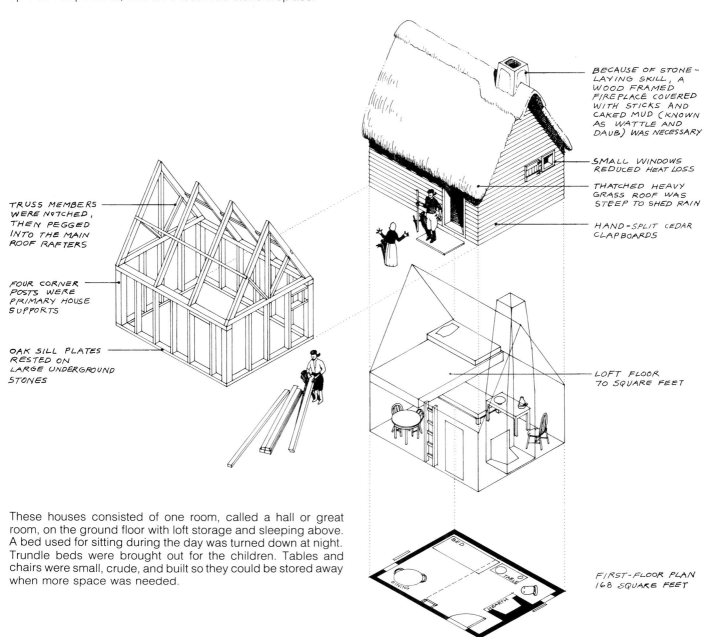

TRUSS MEMBERS WERE NOTCHED, THEN PEGGED INTO THE MAIN ROOF RAFTERS

FOUR CORNER POSTS WERE PRIMARY HOUSE SUPPORTS

OAK SILL PLATES RESTED ON LARGE UNDERGROUND STONES

BECAUSE OF STONE-LAYING SKILL, A WOOD FRAMED FIREPLACE COVERED WITH STICKS AND CAKED MUD (KNOWN AS WATTLE AND DAUB) WAS NECESSARY

SMALL WINDOWS REDUCED HEAT LOSS

THATCHED HEAVY GRASS ROOF WAS STEEP TO SHED RAIN

HAND-SPLIT CEDAR CLAPBOARDS

LOFT FLOOR 70 SQUARE FEET

FIRST-FLOOR PLAN 168 SQUARE FEET

These houses consisted of one room, called a hall or great room, on the ground floor with loft storage and sleeping above. A bed used for sitting during the day was turned down at night. Trundle beds were brought out for the children. Tables and chairs were small, crude, and built so they could be stored away when more space was needed.

Overlapping grass sheaves made up the thatched roof. Supported by a framework of roof rafters, they were tied individually to stick battens for strength and durability. This worked remarkably well in shedding rain, but the dry grass was flammable and provided poor insulation. This type roof is still used on many English homes. The frame shown below evolved over hundreds of years of English homebuilding. Its modern post-and-beam counterpart is basically the same.

The first cottages were quite crude. The floor was dirt, the chimney a fire hazard (some of the houses had no chimney at all, just an opening in the thatched roof), and windows closed only by shutter. Nevertheless, the timber frame structure was to remain the most popular wood building system in America until the invention of the balloon frame in the mid-nineteenth century.

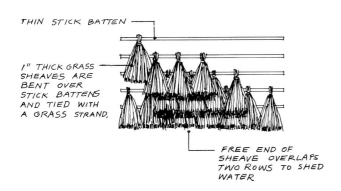

THIN STICK BATTEN

1" THICK GRASS SHEAVES ARE BENT OVER STICK BATTENS AND TIED WITH A GRASS STRAND.

FREE END OF SHEAVE OVERLAPS TWO ROWS TO SHED WATER

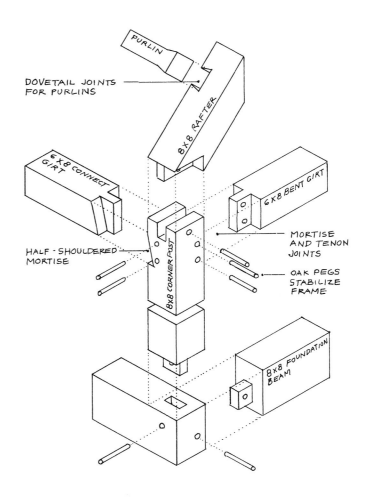

PURLIN

DOVETAIL JOINTS FOR PURLINS

8X8 RAFTER

6X8 CONNECT GIRT

6X8 BENT GIRT

MORTISE AND TENON JOINTS

HALF-SHOULDERED MORTISE

8X8 CORNER POST

OAK PEGS STABILIZE FRAME

8X8 FOUNDATION BEAM

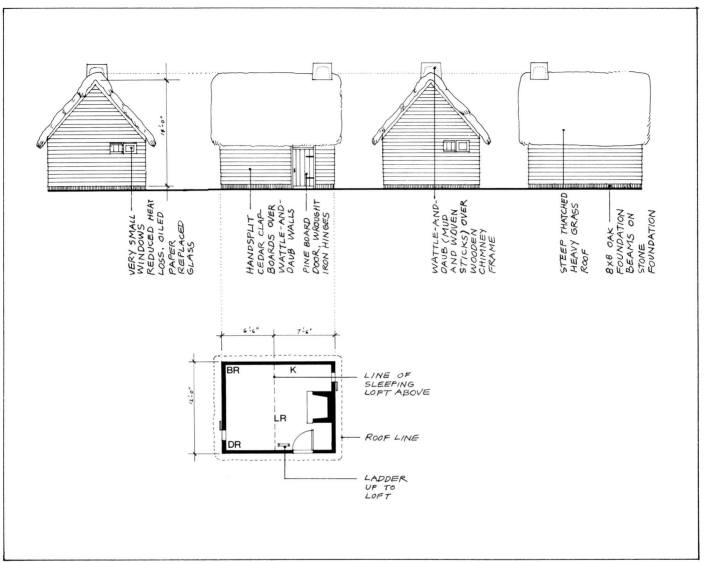

VERY SMALL WINDOWS REDUCED HEAT LOSS, OILED PAPER REPLACED GLASS

HANDSPLIT CEDAR CLAPBOARDS OVER WATTLE-AND-DAUB WALLS

PINE BOARD DOOR, WROUGHT IRON HINGES

WATTLE-AND-DAUB (MUD AND WOVEN STICKS) OVER WOODEN CHIMNEY FRAME

STEEP THATCHED HEAVY GRASS ROOF

8X8 OAK FOUNDATION BEAMS ON STONE FOUNDATION

LINE OF SLEEPING LOFT ABOVE

ROOF LINE

LADDER UP TO LOFT

Plans and Elevations

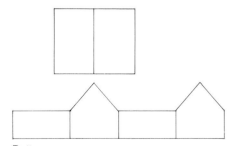

Pattern

Monticello, Virginia

Thomas Jefferson's Honeymoon Cottage

15' x 14' plus unused second floor
210 square feet

During the thirteen years that it took Thomas Jefferson to build his famous Virginia home Monticello, he lived in a small brick building at the end of the south pavilion. Jefferson specifically had this part of Monticello completed first so that he would have a place to live while he supervised the construction of his new home.

He moved into his temporary quarters on November 26, 1770, and described it then in a letter to James Ogilvie: "I have here but one room, which, like the cobler's, serves me for parlour, for

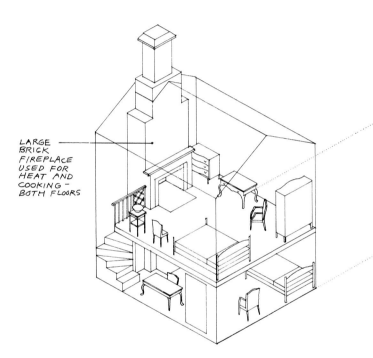

LARGE BRICK FIREPLACE USED FOR HEAT AND COOKING — BOTH FLOORS

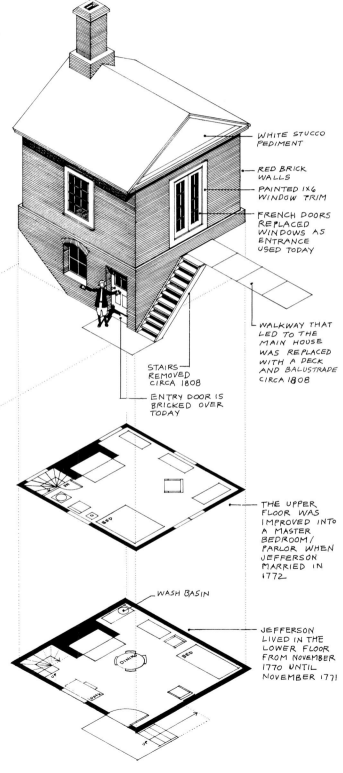

WHITE STUCCO PEDIMENT

RED BRICK WALLS

PAINTED 1x6 WINDOW TRIM

FRENCH DOORS REPLACED WINDOWS AS ENTRANCE USED TODAY

STAIRS REMOVED CIRCA 1808

ENTRY DOOR IS BRICKED OVER TODAY

WALKWAY THAT LED TO THE MAIN HOUSE WAS REPLACED WITH A DECK AND BALUSTRADE CIRCA 1808

THE UPPER FLOOR WAS IMPROVED INTO A MASTER BEDROOM/ PARLOR WHEN JEFFERSON MARRIED IN 1772

WASH BASIN

JEFFERSON LIVED IN THE LOWER FLOOR FROM NOVEMBER 1770 UNTIL NOVEMBER 1771

kitchen and hall. I may add, tor bed chamber and study too. My friends sometimes take a temperate dinner with me and then retire to look for beds elsewhere. I have hopes however of getting more elbow room this summer." It sounds as if the upper room was not yet finished, but it surely was complete a year and a half later, in the spring of 1772, when Jefferson brought his bride, the former Martha Wayles Skelton, there to live.

In this early period of Monticello, the only entrance to the south pavillion "honeymoon cottage" was on the south side of the lower level. The upper ground level was reached by interior or exterior stairs, shown on the drawing above.

It is uncertain when the Jeffersons moved from their honeymoon cottage into the main house, but 1775 would be an educated guess. This would mean that they spent about three and a half years in their tiny house.

When it ceased to be their main home, the Jeffersons used the basement as part of the kitchen serving the main house, and the upper level became a schoolroom. Later it was used as living space for family members and law offices for sons-in-law or grandsons-in-law.

A unique feature of the Jefferson honeymoon cottage is the winding stair built in a space 4'6" x 2'3" wide, illustrated below. The risers are very steep and the space tight but the stair works well. It is practically the same as those stairs built in the brick bandbox townhouses in Philadelphia (see page 32) during the same period.

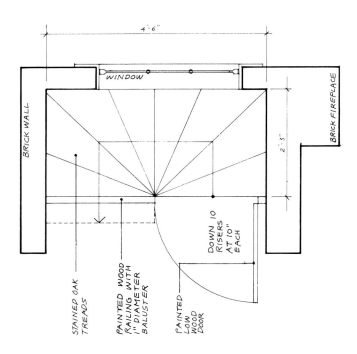

Stair Plan

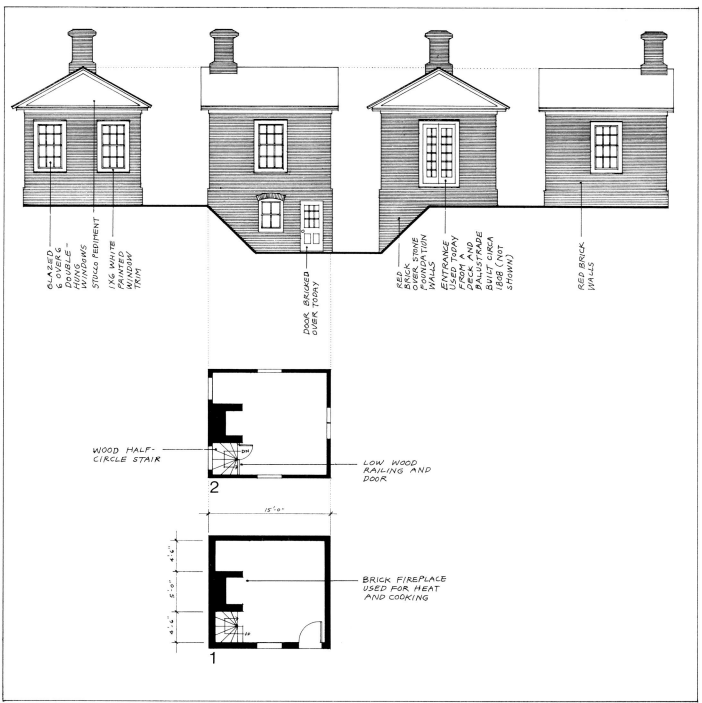

GLAZED 6 OVER 6 DOUBLE-HUNG WINDOWS

STUCCO PEDIMENT

1X6 WHITE PAINTED WINDOW TRIM

DOOR BRICKED OVER TODAY

RED BRICK OVER STONE FOUNDATION WALLS

ENTRANCE USED TODAY FROM A DECK AND BALUSTRADE BUILT CIRCA 1808 (NOT SHOWN)

RED BRICK WALLS

WOOD HALF-CIRCLE STAIR

LOW WOOD RAILING AND DOOR

2

15'-0"

4'-6"

5'-0"

4'-6"

BRICK FIREPLACE USED FOR HEAT AND COOKING

1

Plans and Elevations

The honeymoon cottage was a simple four-wall, gable-roofed structure adapted to the classical style Jefferson planned for Monticello. The classical pediment, white trim, brick walls, and massive brick chimney are details that foreshadowed the Monticello character.

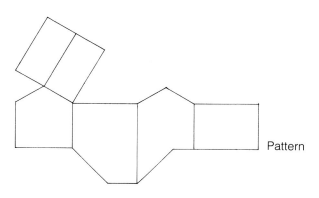

Pattern

Frontier Cabin

16' x 14' plus sleeping attic
224 square feet

Among America's most interesting tiny houses from an an-
thropological point of view are the log cabins built first by
Swedish settlers and later by frontiersmen and traders throughout the country. The cabin shown here is a perfect one-room
portrayal of frontier living quarters built about 1800 in Grainger
County, Tennessee. Now part of the Museum of Appalachia in
Norris, Tennessee, it is known as the Arnwine Cabin, named
after its original owner, John Wesley Arnwine and his family. It
is included in the National Register of Historic Places.

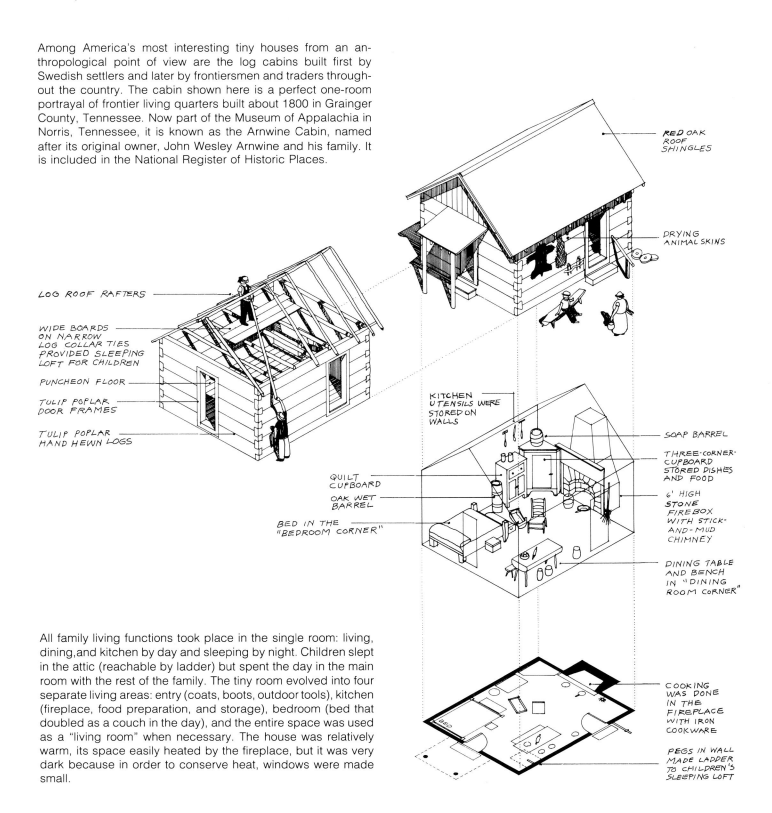

RED OAK ROOF SHINGLES

DRYING ANIMAL SKINS

LOG ROOF RAFTERS

WIDE BOARDS ON NARROW LOG COLLAR TIES PROVIDED SLEEPING LOFT FOR CHILDREN

PUNCHEON FLOOR

TULIP POPLAR DOOR FRAMES

TULIP POPLAR HAND HEWN LOGS

KITCHEN UTENSILS WERE STORED ON WALLS

SOAP BARREL

THREE-CORNER-CUPBOARD STORED DISHES AND FOOD

QUILT CUPBOARD

OAK WET BARREL

6' HIGH STONE FIREBOX WITH STICK-AND-MUD CHIMNEY

BED IN THE "BEDROOM CORNER"

DINING TABLE AND BENCH IN "DINING ROOM CORNER"

COOKING WAS DONE IN THE FIREPLACE WITH IRON COOKWARE

PEGS IN WALL MADE LADDER TO CHILDREN'S SLEEPING LOFT

BED

All family living functions took place in the single room: living,
dining, and kitchen by day and sleeping by night. Children slept
in the attic (reachable by ladder) but spent the day in the main
room with the rest of the family. The tiny room evolved into four
separate living areas: entry (coats, boots, outdoor tools), kitchen
(fireplace, food preparation, and storage), bedroom (bed that
doubled as a couch in the day), and the entire space was used
as a "living room" when necessary. The house was relatively
warm, its space easily heated by the fireplace, but it was very
dark because in order to conserve heat, windows were made
small.

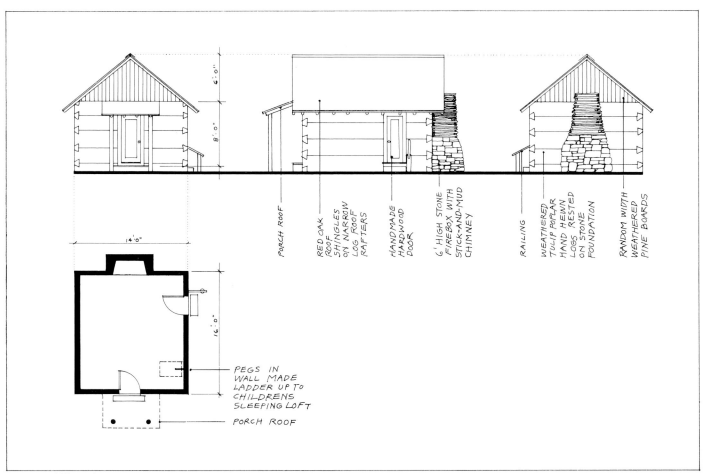

PORCH ROOF

RED OAK ROOF SHINGLES ON NARROW LOG ROOF RAFTERS

HANDMADE HARDWOOD DOOR

6' HIGH STONE FIREBOX WITH STICK-AND-MUD CHIMNEY

RAILING

WEATHERED TULIP POPLAR HAND HEWN LOGS RESTED ON STONE FOUNDATION

RANDOM WIDTH WEATHERED PINE BOARDS

PEGS IN WALL MADE LADDER UP TO CHILDRENS SLEEPING LOFT

PORCH ROOF

Plans and Elevations

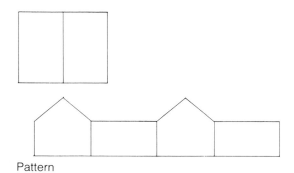

Pattern

Except for the stone fireplace, the interior was constructed from logs, hewn to perform their specific function. Log cabins built today are apt to have more windows, at least in the doors.

Bandbox Townhouse

10' x 10' three stories
300 square feet

The tiniest townhouses in America were built in Philadelphia, Pennsylvania, in the eighteenth and nineteenth centuries. Constructed on speculation as tenant houses for immigrants, they were three stories high, with one room of about 100 square feet on each floor. These houses were called "bandbox houses" when they were built but today they're known as "Trinity houses" because of their three floors. They were often built in two groups of two or four, facing a common cul-de-sac courtyard, perpendicular to the street. There were usually four common wooden outhouses located at the end of the court, opposite the entrance.

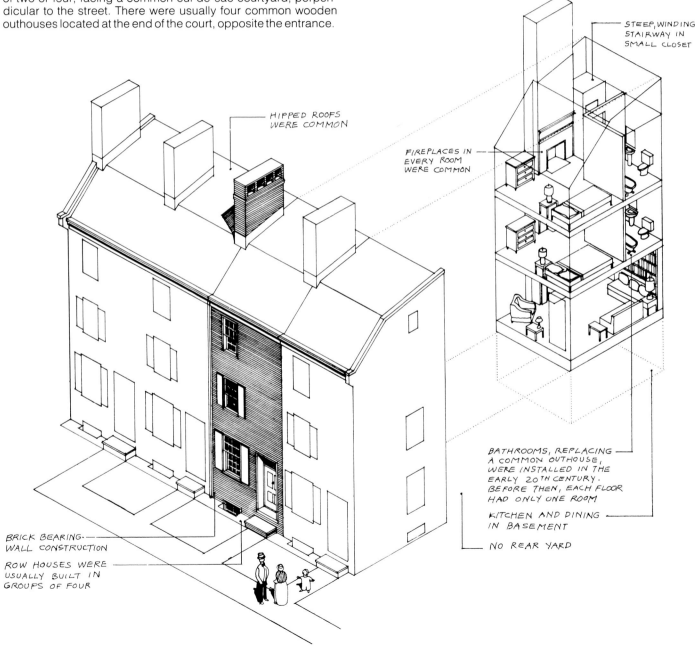

STEEP, WINDING STAIRWAY IN SMALL CLOSET

HIPPED ROOFS WERE COMMON

FIREPLACES IN EVERY ROOM WERE COMMON

BATHROOMS, REPLACING A COMMON OUTHOUSE, WERE INSTALLED IN THE EARLY 20TH CENTURY. BEFORE THEN, EACH FLOOR HAD ONLY ONE ROOM

KITCHEN AND DINING IN BASEMENT

NO REAR YARD

BRICK BEARING WALL CONSTRUCTION

ROW HOUSES WERE USUALLY BUILT IN GROUPS OF FOUR

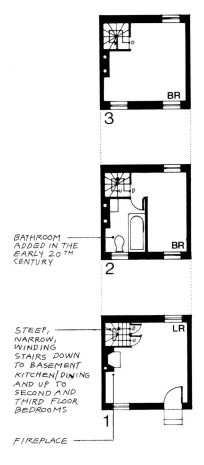

BATHROOM
ADDED IN THE
EARLY 20TH
CENTURY

STEEP,
NARROW,
WINDING
STAIRS DOWN
TO BASEMENT
KITCHEN/DINING
AND UP TO
SECOND AND
THIRD FLOOR
BEDROOMS

FIREPLACE

The bandbox floor plan is quite simple. Three blocks of space stacked one on top of the other with all the services, fireplaces, and stairs located on the common wall opposite the entrance. The brick bearing walls with wood joists span the 10- to 16-foot width between apartments.

Cape Cod Honeymoon Cottage

18' x 16' plus sleeping attic
288 square feet

The quintessential in romantic tiny houses is the original honeymoon cottage version of the well-known Cape Cod house. During the eighteenth century, when young settlers were inhabiting the Cape Cod area, they built half-sized or partially built Cape Cod houses and added to them as their families grew and their wealth increased.

CEDAR SHAKE SHINGLE ROOF

WEATHERED CEDAR SHINGLES

TIE BEAMS SERVED AS FLOOR SUPPORTS FOR SLEEPING LOFT

FOUR CORNER POSTS WERE PRIMARY HOUSE SUPPORTS

10X10 OAK SILL PLATES

PICKET FENCE GUARDED AGAINST SHIFTING SANDS

LARGE STONE FIREPLACE USED FOR HEAT AND COOKING

The original design was a simple gable-roofed structure built with an oversized frame on huge 10" x 10" oak sills. As the dunes shifted, ship's carpenters used teams of horses to drag the houses across the sand to more desirable sites. Eighteen-inch-wide vertical planks provided an ingenious means of both stabilizing the post-and-beam frame and of sheathing the native cedar shingles on the outside and plaster on the inside. The outside of the Cape Cod has no projections or extraneous decoration that might prove vulnerable to ocean gale-force winds.

Inside, the rooms were clustered around a large brick chimney that opened into a fireplace used for cooking, heating, and light. The attic was partitioned into small bedrooms with windows in the gable end of the building.

7'x9' BEDROOM HAS SPACE FOR DOUBLE BED

STEEP STAIR UP TO SLEEPING LOFT

35

The Cape Cod was inventively designed so it could expand when the family grew larger. The one-half Cape Cod was the "honeymoon cottage." The three-quarter Cape Cod was the answer when children first arrived, and the full Cape Cod was used for a large family.

The drawing below shows a modern development of the Cape Cod plan. Earlier ones would have a fireplace in the kitchen for cooking and in the dining room (known as the parlor in the eighteenth century) for heating.

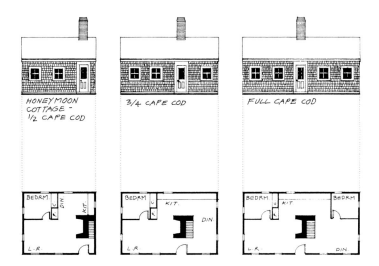

HONEYMOON COTTAGE - 1/2 CAPE COD

3/4 CAPE COD

FULL CAPE COD

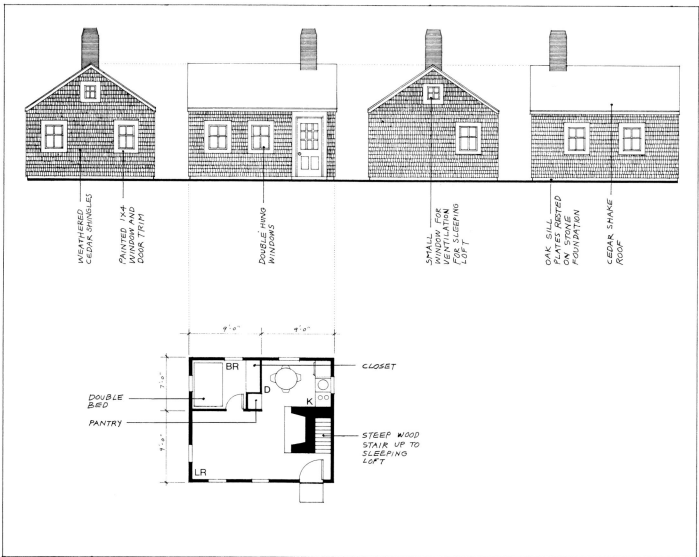

Plans and Elevations

Labels on the elevations:
WEATHERED CEDAR SHINGLES
PAINTED 1X4 WINDOW AND DOOR TRIM
DOUBLE HUNG WINDOWS
SMALL WINDOW FOR VENTILATION FOR SLEEPING LOFT
OAK SILL PLATES RESTED ON STONE FOUNDATION
CEDAR SHAKE ROOF

Labels on the plan:
9'0"   9'0"
7'0"   9'0"
BR
CLOSET
D
DOUBLE BED
PANTRY
K
LR
STEEP WOOD STAIR UP TO SLEEPING LOFT

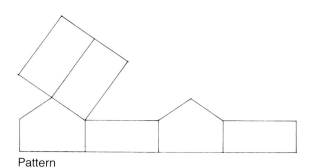

Pattern

The Cape Cod was originally a fisherman's cottage, built in the vernacular style, with local materials allowed to weather. During the 1940s and 1950s and 1960s it was extremely popular with the prefabricating home industry because of its simple shape and romantic past. The most commonly built house in America, the Cape Cod makes for a perfect tiny vacation home or honeymoon cottage.

Henry Thoreau's Cabin

15' x 10' plus root cellar and attic
150 square feet

Beginning in late March of 1845, Henry David Thoreau built a tiny house on the shore of Walden Pond in Concord, Massachusetts, at a cost of $28.12½. He spent two years in this cabin, built with his own hands, while proving his famous experiment—that man could live happily and independently of other men. In his book *Walden*, Thoreau left a complete description of his house (including a materials list, dimensions, building techniques, and cost) that has enabled the reconstruction of many exact replicas by Thoreau admirers.

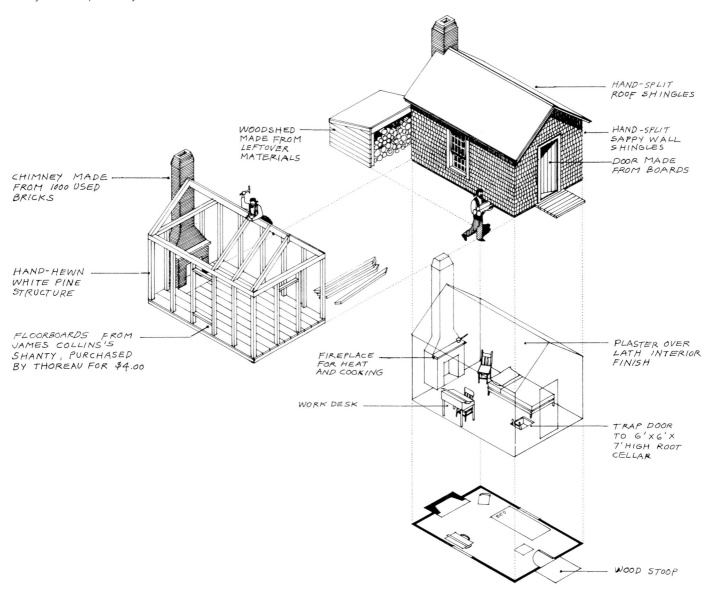

HAND-SPLIT ROOF SHINGLES

HAND-SPLIT SAPPY WALL SHINGLES

DOOR MADE FROM BOARDS

WOODSHED MADE FROM LEFTOVER MATERIALS

CHIMNEY MADE FROM 1000 USED BRICKS

HAND-HEWN WHITE PINE STRUCTURE

FLOORBOARDS FROM JAMES COLLINS'S SHANTY, PURCHASED BY THOREAU FOR $4.00

FIREPLACE FOR HEAT AND COOKING

WORK DESK

PLASTER OVER LATH INTERIOR FINISH

TRAP DOOR TO 6'X6'X 7'HIGH ROOT CELLAR

WOOD STOOP

The most interesting aspect of the Thoreau Cabin is the frame. Thoreau economized on the work required to build a squared frame by hewing only the necessary edges of each frame member.

"Near the end of March, 1845, I borrowed an axe and went down to the woods by Walden Pond, nearest to where I intended to build my house, and began to cut down some tall, arrowy white pines, still in their youth, for timber."

"So I went on for some days cutting and hewing timber, and also studding and rafters."

"I hewed the main timbers six inches square, most of the studs on two sides only, and the rafters and floor timbers on one side, leaving the rest of the bark on, so that they were just as straight and much stronger than sawed ones. Each stick was carefully mortised and tenoned by its stump, for I had borrowed other tools by this time."

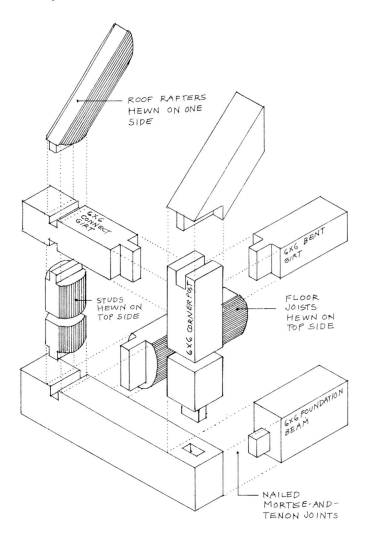

ROOF RAFTERS HEWN ON ONE SIDE

6X6 CONNECT GIRT

6X6 BENT GIRT

STUDS HEWN ON TOP SIDE

6X6 CORNER POST

FLOOR JOISTS HEWN ON TOP SIDE

6X6 FOUNDATION BEAM

NAILED MORTISE-AND-TENON JOINTS

"By the middle of April, for I had made no haste in my work, but rather made the most of it, my house was framed and ready for the raising."

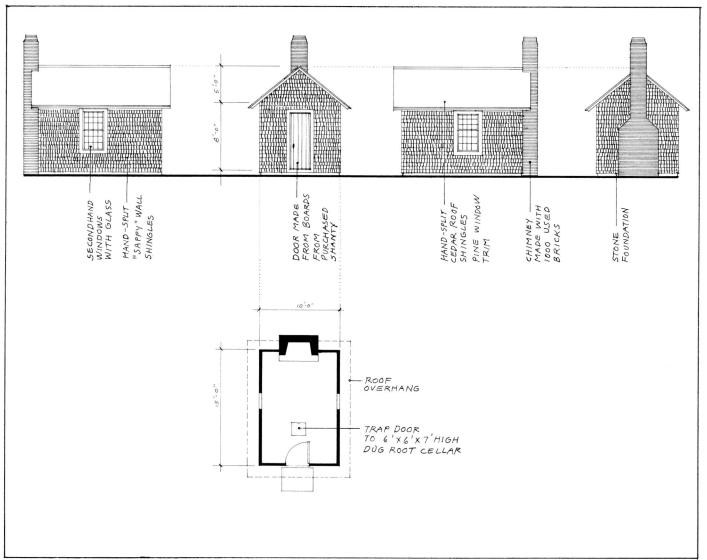

Plans and Elevations

Labels on elevations (left to right):
- SECONDHAND WINDOWS WITH GLASS
- HAND-SPLIT "SAPPY" WALL SHINGLES
- DOOR MADE FROM BOARDS FROM PURCHASED SHANTY
- HAND-SPLIT CEDAR ROOF SHINGLES
- PINE WINDOW TRIM
- CHIMNEY MADE WITH 1000 USED BRICKS
- STONE FOUNDATION

Plan labels:
- ROOF OVERHANG
- TRAP DOOR TO 6' x 6' x 7' HIGH DUG ROOT CELLAR

Dimensions: 5'-0", 8'-0", 10'-0", 15'-0"

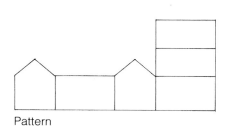

Pattern

Thoreau moved into his house on the Fourth of July, 1845, but continued to work on it as time permitted.

"I built the chimney after my hoeing in the fall, before a fire became necessary for warmth, doing my cooking in the meanwhile out of doors on the ground, early in the morning."

**

—quotes from *Walden* (See Bibliography)

Thoreau finally completed his house by plastering the interior on November 12, 1845.

The house's shape, construction, and heating system are very basic and straightforward. It would be one of the most pleasurable of the tiny houses in this book to build from scratch and would be a wise choice for beginners.

Circa 1890

Circa 1950

Daniel Ricketson's Shanty

14' x 12'
168 square feet

Daniel Ricketson was a dilettante famed for his friendships with some of the nineteenth century's greats, such as reformer Theodore Parker, author John Greenleaf Whittier, and most memorably, with the Concord Transcendentalists, Henry David Thoreau and Ralph Waldo Emerson. After reading Thoreau's *Walden*, published in 1854, Ricketson was so impressed that he decided to have a carpenter build him a "shanty" similar to Thoreau's, near his home in Brooklawn, Massachusetts.

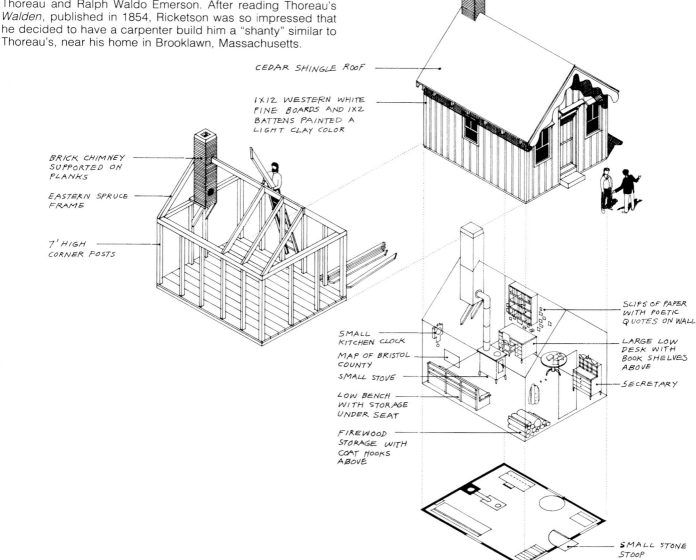

CEDAR SHINGLE ROOF

1X12 WESTERN WHITE PINE BOARDS AND 1X2 BATTENS PAINTED A LIGHT CLAY COLOR

BRICK CHIMNEY SUPPORTED ON PLANKS

EASTERN SPRUCE FRAME

7' HIGH CORNER POSTS

SMALL KITCHEN CLOCK

MAP OF BRISTOL COUNTY

SMALL STOVE

LOW BENCH WITH STORAGE UNDER SEAT

FIREWOOD STORAGE WITH COAT HOOKS ABOVE

SLIPS OF PAPER WITH POETIC QUOTES ON WALL

LARGE LOW DESK WITH BOOK SHELVES ABOVE

SECRETARY

SMALL STONE STOOP

An accurate description of the Ricketson Shanty can be found in Henry Thoreau's *Journal* as he wrote about it after a visit there on April 10, 1857. After painfully listing every piece of furniture and other contents within the shanty, Thoreau stated, "I found all his peculiarities faithfully expressed, his humanity, his fear of death, love of retirement, simplicity, etc."

The house is included in this book because it is simple, easy to build, interestingly influenced by Thoreau's cabin, and an expression of a mid-nineteenth-century character's life.

The most interesting part of the Ricketson Shanty is the decoration. In 1857, scroll-sawn barge boards were becoming very popular on houses throughout America. They are still very easy to make and install if you have a few extra hours and wish to express yourself as did Daniel Ricketson.

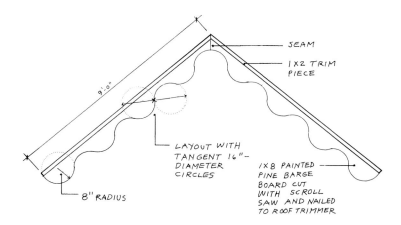

SEAM

1 X 2 TRIM PIECE

9'-0"

LAYOUT WITH TANGENT 16"- DIAMETER CIRCLES

1 X 8 PAINTED PINE BARGE BOARD CUT WITH SCROLL SAW AND NAILED TO ROOF TRIMMER

8" RADIUS

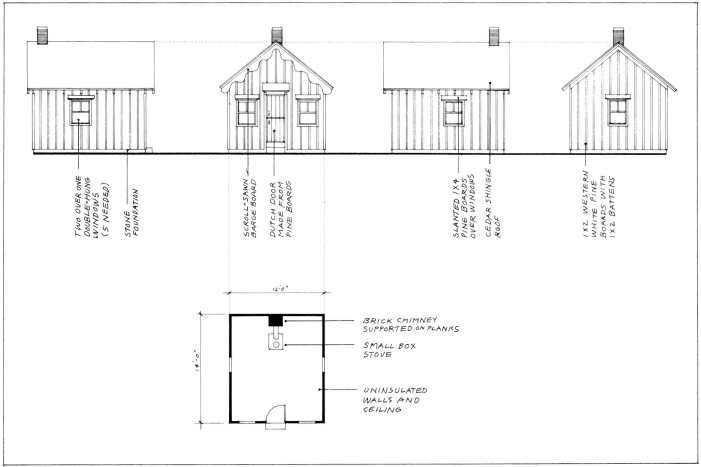

TWO OVER ONE
DOUBLE-HUNG
WINDOWS
(5 NEEDED)

STONE
FOUNDATION

SCROLL-SAWN
BARGE BOARD

DUTCH DOOR
MADE FROM
PINE BOARDS

SLANTED 1X4
PINE BOARDS
OVER WINDOWS

CEDAR SHINGLE
ROOF

1X2 WESTERN
WHITE PINE
BOARDS WITH
1X2 BATTENS

12'-0"

14'-0"

BRICK CHIMNEY
SUPPORTED ON PLANKS

SMALL BOX
STOVE

UNINSULATED
WALLS AND
CEILING

Plans and Elevations

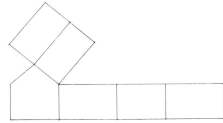

Pattern

Unlike Thoreau's straightforward woodsmanlike methods, Ricketson's technique was affected by the new architectural style sweeping the country at the time—the "cottage style," espoused by A. J. Downing in his popular book *The Architecture of Country Houses*, published in 1850. Board-and-batten siding, to emphasize the vertical line, and gingerbread barge boards, hallmarks of this early Victorian style, were incorporated by Ricketson in his otherwise simple shanty. One can only imagine Thoreau's expression as he viewed the Ricketson Shanty with its decorative affectations, knowing that it was conceived as an "updated" version of his own.

Campground Cottage

19'-6" x 11'-4" plus sleeping attic
221 square feet

In the mid-nineteenth century, America was dotted with Methodist camp-meeting grounds where religious revivals, lasting several days, would occur regularly. (By 1875 there were eight permanent campgrounds spaced across Massachusetts alone.) Revivalists would arrive at one of these sites, rent a tent, dine and wash communally, and participate in religious meetings held in a clearing surrounded by tents.

The largest of these Methodist campgrounds is Wesleyan Grove in Oak Bluffs (named Cottage City until 1907), Martha's Vineyard, off the coast of Cape Cod, Massachusetts. The special resort qualities of the island and its close proximity to large urban areas caused the Wesleyan Grove campground to grow almost overnight. In 1840, eight hundred people attended weekly meetings with two thousand more arriving just for Sunday services. By 1858, over twelve thousand people were attending the Sunday meeting in what was proclaimed to be the largest camp meeting in the world. The tents had evolved into canvas-topped, wood-sided, wood-framed, candlelit structures that glowed at night, further enhancing the religious ambiance of the community. Church correspondents called it a "celestial city."

By 1864, forty tiny prefabricated Carpenter Gothic wooden houses had been built, sprinkled among five hundred canvas and wood-sided tents, constructed on their original tent platforms. For the next decade, every year fifteen to fifty new wooden cottages replaced the tents, each with more elaborate Carpenter Gothic ornamentation than the next. Today three hundred twenty beautifully preserved wooden cottages remain. Most have rear kitchen and bath additions, and fifty-two are winterized and occupied year-round.

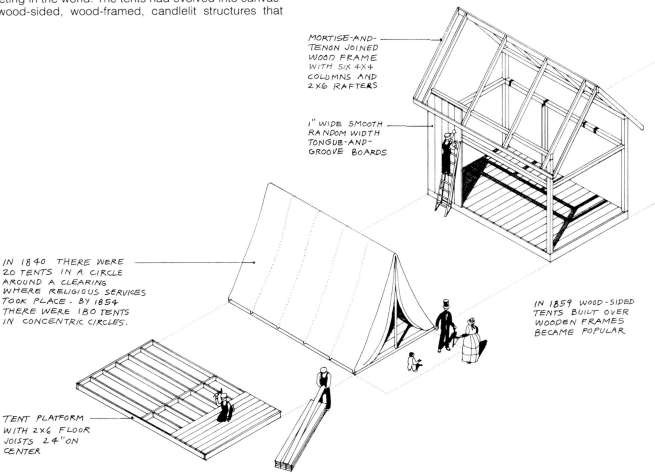

MORTISE-AND-TENON JOINED WOOD FRAME WITH SIX 4X4 COLUMNS AND 2X6 RAFTERS

1" WIDE SMOOTH RANDOM WIDTH TONGUE-AND-GROOVE BOARDS

IN 1840 THERE WERE 20 TENTS IN A CIRCLE AROUND A CLEARING WHERE RELIGIOUS SERVICES TOOK PLACE. BY 1854 THERE WERE 180 TENTS IN CONCENTRIC CIRCLES.

IN 1859 WOOD-SIDED TENTS BUILT OVER WOODEN FRAMES BECAME POPULAR

TENT PLATFORM WITH 2X6 FLOOR JOISTS 24" ON CENTER

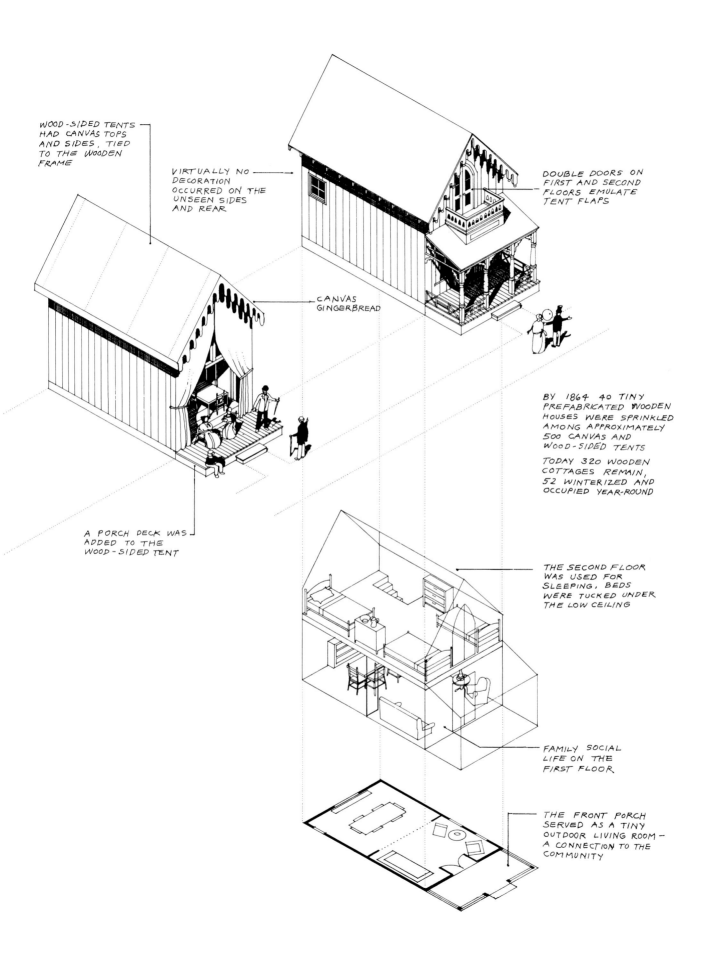

WOOD-SIDED TENTS HAD CANVAS TOPS AND SIDES, TIED TO THE WOODEN FRAME

VIRTUALLY NO DECORATION OCCURRED ON THE UNSEEN SIDES AND REAR

CANVAS GINGERBREAD

A PORCH DECK WAS ADDED TO THE WOOD-SIDED TENT

DOUBLE DOORS ON FIRST AND SECOND FLOORS EMULATE TENT FLAPS

BY 1864 40 TINY PREFABRICATED WOODEN HOUSES WERE SPRINKLED AMONG APPROXIMATELY 500 CANVAS AND WOOD-SIDED TENTS

TODAY 320 WOODEN COTTAGES REMAIN, 52 WINTERIZED AND OCCUPIED YEAR-ROUND

THE SECOND FLOOR WAS USED FOR SLEEPING, BEDS WERE TUCKED UNDER THE LOW CEILING

FAMILY SOCIAL LIFE ON THE FIRST FLOOR

THE FRONT PORCH SERVED AS A TINY OUTDOOR LIVING ROOM – A CONNECTION TO THE COMMUNITY

47

Circa 1860

By 1859, wood-sided tents had reached their peak, numbering well over four hundred. Many were quite refined and decorative in appearance and were, of course, an interesting link between the first plain canvas tents and the classic Carpenter Gothic cottages that exist today.

Circa 1870

The first elaborate Gothic cottage was prefabricated in Providence, Rhode Island, shipped to Martha's Vineyard, and erected in three days in 1859. By 1864 six local builders were prefabricating the cottages in quantity in nearby Edgartown. Forty cottages were built that year at costs ranging from $150 to $600.

The tiniest, most popular campground cottages are simple rectangular, gable-roofed structures, 11'-4" wide and 19'-6" deep, one-and-a-half stories high. The gable is always to the front, and double doors open like tent flaps into the first-floor room. Front porches were added twenty to thirty years after most cottages were constructed.

Because the cottages are often grouped closely together, most of the ornamentation is oriented toward the front, and it is there that a hundred-year "gingerbread" competition has been waged. Over forty-five different decoration patterns have been counted and, with the endless variety of window and door types, balconies, porches, shutters, and wall treatments, all using the Carpenter Gothic vocabulary, a seemingly infinite amount of delicate tiny houses has been built. Today the competition centers around color, bright, high-gloss, attention-getting colors in combinations never dreamed of: one house is two shades of day-glo pink, another is purple and white.

As one walks around this tiny colorful village on paths draped with huge elm and sycamore trees, one is struck with how perfect the place is for neighborhood living. Because the houses are little and their colors bright, there is a strong sense of community identity. Because of the tiny scale, trees seems larger, nature seems larger, the car and other machines seem out of place, and people seem very important.

Many of the cottages have distinctive front doors in round-headed shapes with double doors repeating themselves on the attic facade above. These Gothic-style doors were used to get bedroom furniture into the second floor because the interior stair was so small.

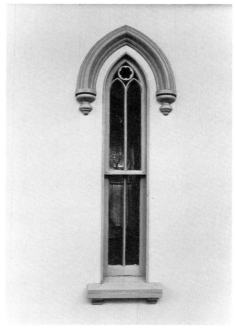

Many campground cottages used the popular Carpenter Gothic board-and-batten siding to emphasize the vertical line. But many more, as pictured above, used flush vertical boards to simulate a cut-stone facade, popular with the Early Gothic Revival style in the 1840s.

At the turn of the century, some of the campground cottages were connected together with wooden walkways—an interesting expression of community. Private second-floor cantilevered balconies were common.

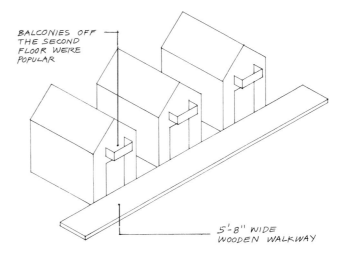

BALCONIES OFF
THE SECOND
FLOOR WERE
POPULAR

5'-8" WIDE
WOODEN WALKWAY

In the 1920s and 1930s private porches were built facing the community pathway. These porches created a protected outdoor living space, a kind of soft buffer between the private living room and the public outdoors.

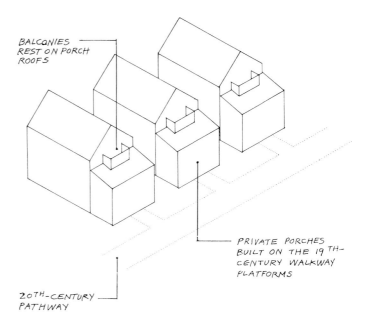

BALCONIES REST ON PORCH ROOFS

PRIVATE PORCHES BUILT ON THE 19TH-CENTURY WALKWAY PLATFORMS

20TH-CENTURY PATHWAY

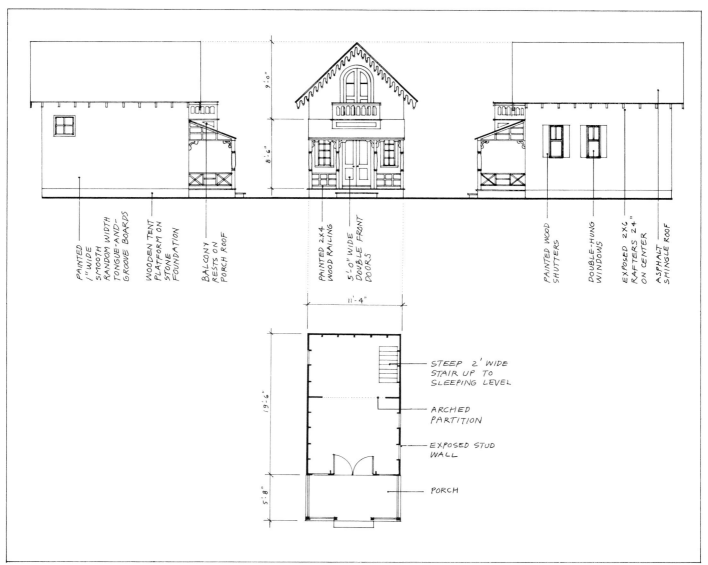

PAINTED 1" WIDE SMOOTH RANDOM WIDTH TONGUE-AND-GROOVE BOARDS

WOODEN TENT PLATFORM ON STONE FOUNDATION

BALCONY RESTS ON PORCH ROOF

PAINTED 2×4 WOOD RAILING

5'-0" WIDE DOUBLE FRONT DOORS

PAINTED WOOD SHUTTERS

DOUBLE-HUNG WINDOWS

EXPOSED 2×6 RAFTERS 24" ON CENTER

ASPHALT SHINGLE ROOF

9'-0"

8'-6"

11'-4"

19'-6"

5'-8"

STEEP 2' WIDE STAIR UP TO SLEEPING LEVEL

ARCHED PARTITION

EXPOSED STUD WALL

PORCH

Plans and Elevations

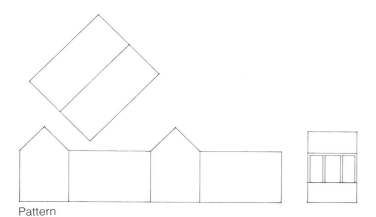

Pattern

The prototypical campground cottage plan evolved from that of the tents, with a larger room in the front, separated from a smaller room behind by a decorative arched partition. This second room contained a narrow stair that led to the upper sleeping level. Originally, kitchens and outhouses were separated from the cottages. During the early part of the twentieth century, small kitchens and bathrooms were added to the rear of the cottages but they had little effect on the livability of the plan.

In 1869 another significant Methodist camp-meeting ground was started in Ocean Grove, on the New Jersey shore near Asbury Park. As with Martha's Vineyard and Pacific Grove in California, this site was selected for its convenience and the beauty of its landscape.

In 1894 the "Great Auditorium," a huge building that seated over six thousand, was completed. It became a symbolic center for a community that to this day remains committed to its religion and austere life-style. By the turn of the century, many worshipers were visiting every summer, and what began as a small grouping of tents circling the Great Auditorium had evolved into a tent city with over two hundred fifty very distinctive, innovative tiny tent buildings.

The tents were built by the Ocean Grove Camp Meeting Association and leased to families for a full summer season, usually lasting from May until September. They consist of a canvas-covered porch, an 11' x 14' canvas living-sleeping room, and an 11' x 14' wooden section with kitchen, bath, and dining area built behind the tent structure. During the winter, the canvas is removed from its platform and stored in the wooden building. The total square footage of the complete summertime structure, both wood and canvas sections, is three hundred eight.

Today, one hundred fourteen of these tent houses still exist and many of them are still being leased by their original families. In 1985, all the tents were reconstructed by the Foster Awning Company of Neptune, New Jersey, to meet local fire codes. There is a five-year waiting list for the use of these houses.

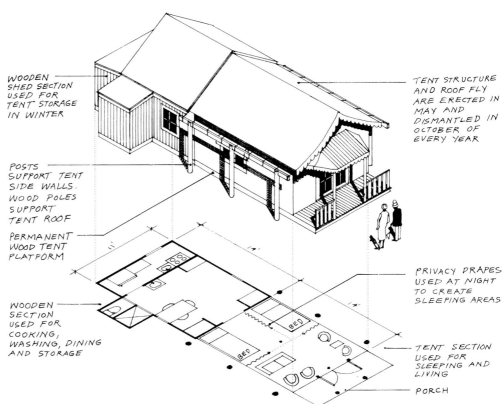

WOODEN SHED SECTION USED FOR TENT STORAGE IN WINTER

POSTS SUPPORT TENT SIDE WALLS. WOOD POLES SUPPORT TENT ROOF

PERMANENT WOOD TENT PLATFORM

WOODEN SECTION USED FOR COOKING, WASHING, DINING AND STORAGE

TENT STRUCTURE AND ROOF FLY ARE ERECTED IN MAY AND DISMANTLED IN OCTOBER OF EVERY YEAR

PRIVACY DRAPES USED AT NIGHT TO CREATE SLEEPING AREAS

TENT SECTION USED FOR SLEEPING AND LIVING

PORCH

BED

BED

Chattel House

16' x 15'
240 square feet

The Chattel House on the small Caribbean island of Barbados is one of the most interesting tiny houses in the world. It was built by freed (1833) slave plantation workers who were obliged to rent land in a "tenantry" from the plantation on which they chose to work. Often, on short notice, they were forced to move, and the ability to take their belongings with them meant everything. The house itself was a movable possession—a "chattel."

The chattel house was lightweight, built of wood, and as small as possible so that it could be lifted onto a cart and moved to another location. It rested on three- or four-feet-high coral blocks or, today, concrete blocks, providing a space under the house for cooling air to circulate. The house was usually situated to take advantage of the prevailing easterly breezes, gathered in by hoods over the windows.

The facade of the chattel house is symmetrical, with one window on either side of the centered porch and door, similar to much larger houses built by Barbados planters and merchants. Craftsmanship was excellent because although the land was rented, the houses were owned.

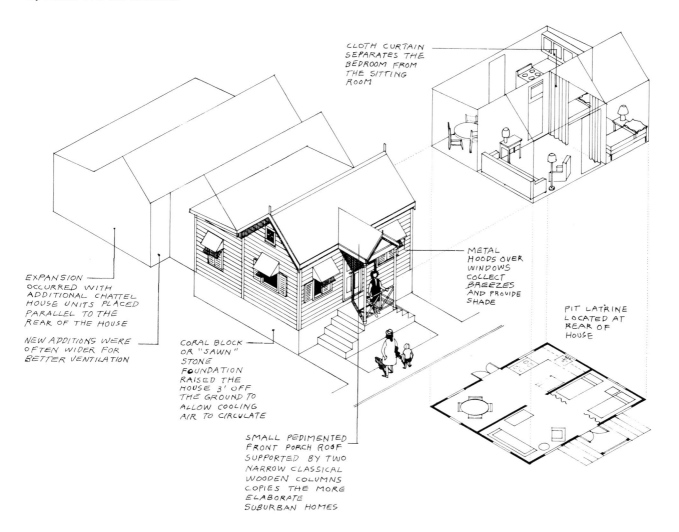

CLOTH CURTAIN SEPARATES THE BEDROOM FROM THE SITTING ROOM

EXPANSION OCCURRED WITH ADDITIONAL CHATTEL HOUSE UNITS PLACED PARALLEL TO THE REAR OF THE HOUSE

NEW ADDITIONS WERE OFTEN WIDER FOR BETTER VENTILATION

CORAL BLOCK OR "SAWN" STONE FOUNDATION RAISED THE HOUSE 3' OFF THE GROUND TO ALLOW COOLING AIR TO CIRCULATE

METAL HOODS OVER WINDOWS COLLECT BREEZES AND PROVIDE SHADE

PIT LATRINE LOCATED AT REAR OF HOUSE

SMALL PEDIMENTED FRONT PORCH ROOF SUPPORTED BY TWO NARROW CLASSICAL WOODEN COLUMNS COPIES THE MORE ELABORATE SUBURBAN HOMES

Larger chattel houses are made by stacking one unit behind the other, each with an increasing width so that front ventilation is possible. Some chattel houses grow to be five or six units deep. The chattel house is a unique building system—beginning small, solving problems of ventilation and space allocation, then adding rooms as time and money permit. It is folk architecture at its best.

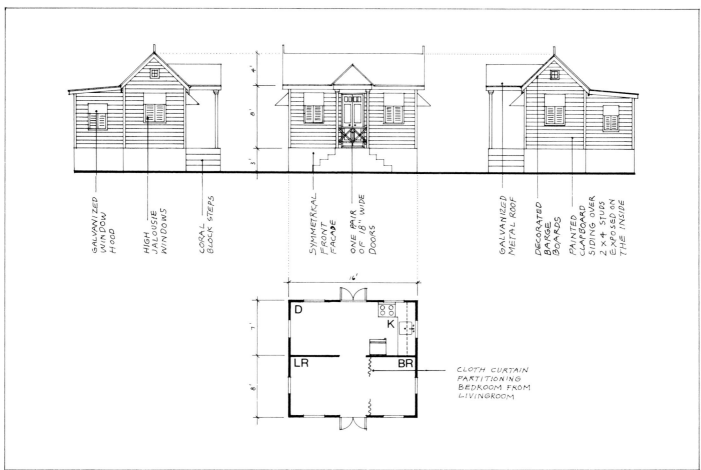

GALVANIZED WINDOW HOOD

HIGH JALOUSIE WINDOWS

CORAL BLOCK STEPS

SYMMETRICAL FRONT FACADE

ONE PAIR OF 18" WIDE DOORS

GALVANIZED METAL ROOF

DECORATED BARGE BOARDS

PAINTED CLAPBOARD SIDING OVER 2 x 4 STUDS EXPOSED ON THE INSIDE

D

K

LR

BR

CLOTH CURTAIN PARTITIONING BEDROOM FROM LIVINGROOM

16'

Plans and Elevations

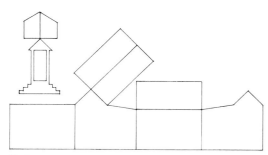

Pattern

The chattel house plan is similar to the American Cape Cod (pages 34-37) where a front entry splits two sitting rooms leading to a lean-to kitchen and dining area at the rear. The chattel house is much smaller in volume than the Cape Cod so that one of the sitting rooms must double as a bedroom (the Cape Cod has attic sleeping).

Windows and doors are placed for maximum ventilation. It is interesting to note that if the house is divided into four rooms with a center hall, all four rooms would have cross ventilation. This house is easy to build with one gable-roofed structure, one lean-to structure, and a front porch. The chattel house would also be fun to craft because it accommodates ornamentation, and the basic plan can adapt to a wide variety of needs and site conditions.

Weber House

Sunday House

14' x 14' plus sleeping attic
196 square feet

The Sunday house was built by the early rural German residents of Gillespie County in Fredericksburg, Texas, for use when they came to town to worship or do their marketing on weekends. These tiny buildings, often no more than a 15' x 15' room with sleeping attic above, were unique to Fredericksburg, and only a few remain. A good example is the one shown here, the Weber House, located on the grounds of the Pioneer Museum on the main street of Fredericksburg.

From the 1880s through the 1920s farmers and ranchers would habitually come to town on Saturday morning to do their marketing and visiting and then went to church and Sunday school on Sunday morning, returning home that evening. The Sunday houses they built were equipped with just the essentials—beds, table and benches, a cupboard, a wood heat/cookstove, perhaps a cot, a rocking chair, and some cooking utensils. If the house was crowded, the adults ate first while the children played outside. When the men had finally taken their conversation to the front porch, the children sat down for *zweiter Tisch*. The Weber House has an outside portable ladder to the children's sleeping attic, but many Sunday houses had outdoor stairs like those illustrated on the following page.

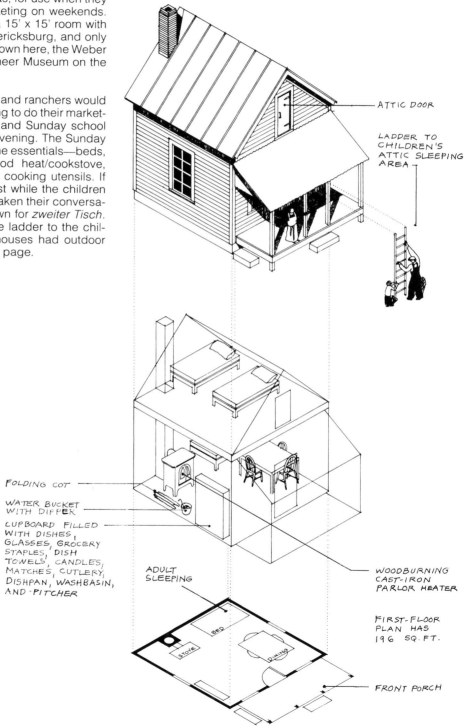

ATTIC DOOR

LADDER TO CHILDREN'S ATTIC SLEEPING AREA

FOLDING COT

WATER BUCKET WITH DIPPER

CUPBOARD FILLED WITH DISHES, GLASSES, GROCERY STAPLES, DISH TOWELS, CANDLES, MATCHES, CUTLERY, DISHPAN, WASHBASIN, AND PITCHER

ADULT SLEEPING

WOODBURNING CAST-IRON PARLOR HEATER

FIRST-FLOOR PLAN HAS 196 SQ. FT.

FRONT PORCH

STOVE

BED

DINING

Each Sunday-house builder carefully considered his needs before he constructed his little town home. If a family lived near town and used the Sunday house only for Sunday dinner, they would build a one-room wood-frame house with a front porch. Large families who traveled fifteen or twenty miles to town in a buggy or wagon often liked the one-and-a-half-story wood-frame house with two compact first-floor rooms and a large sleeping attic above (as illustrated below).

When, around 1920, the automobile quickened the pace of transportation, Sunday houses were no longer needed. Many became retirement homes for older farmers who chose to move into town. They often added lean-to kitchens and bathrooms. For this reason, there are very few Sunday houses left in their original condition.

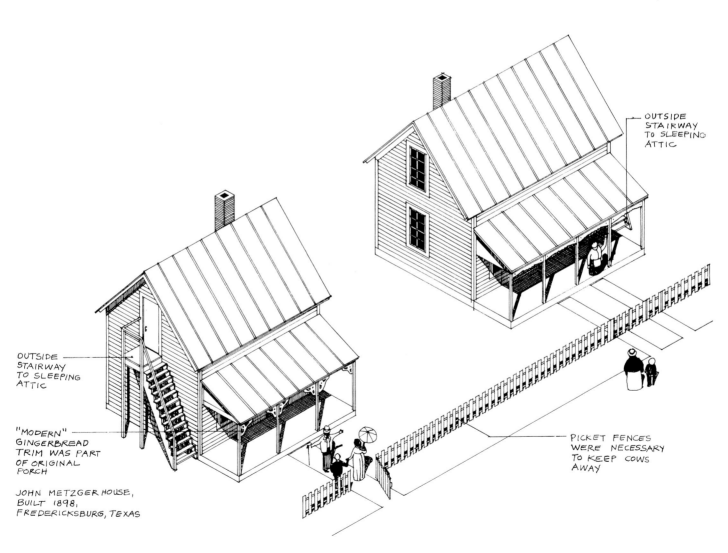

CRISTIAN CRENWELGE PLACE
FREDERICKSBURG, TEXAS

OUTSIDE STAIRWAY TO SLEEPING ATTIC

OUTSIDE STAIRWAY TO SLEEPING ATTIC

"MODERN" GINGERBREAD TRIM WAS PART OF ORIGINAL PORCH

JOHN METZGER HOUSE, BUILT 1898, FREDERICKSBURG, TEXAS

PICKET FENCES WERE NECESSARY TO KEEP COWS AWAY

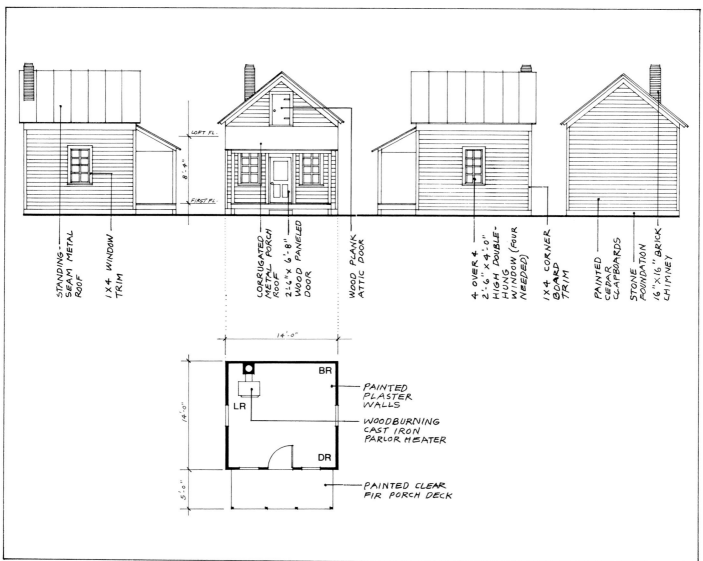

STANDING-SEAM METAL ROOF

1X4 WINDOW TRIM

CORRUGATED METAL PORCH ROOF

2'-6" x 6'-8" WOOD PANELED DOOR

WOOD PLANK ATTIC DOOR

4 OVER 4 2'-6" X 4'-0" HIGH DOUBLE-HUNG WINDOW (FOUR NEEDED)

1X4 CORNER BOARD TRIM

PAINTED CEDAR CLAPBOARDS

STONE FOUNDATION

16"X16" BRICK CHIMNEY

LOFT FL.

8'-4"

FIRST FL.

14'-0"

14'-0"

5'-0"

BR

LR

DR

PAINTED PLASTER WALLS

WOODBURNING CAST IRON PARLOR HEATER

PAINTED CLEAR FIR PORCH DECK

Plans and Elevations

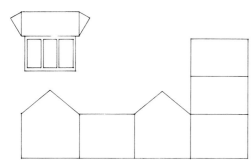

Pattern

Gable-roofed, wood-framed, uninsulated Sunday houses usually rested on a fieldstone foundation slightly elevated above the ground for ventilation. The house had a very simple front porch and a centered front door with a large double-hung window on either side. A small brick chimney rose from the back of the house through the tin roof. Stored near the chimney was the ladder that gave access, over the front porch roof, to the sleeping attic.

Circa 1906   1,652 Type "B" shacks under construction in Camp Richmond

Earthquake Refugee Shack

14' x 10'
140 square feet

In 1906, after the most destructive earthquake in San Francisco history, the United States Army built 5,610 tiny redwood and fir "relief houses" as makeshift homes for twenty thousand refugees. Built with their sides practically touching, they were packed into eleven refugee camps, and rented for two dollars per month until the city was rebuilt. Designed by John McLare, the "Father of Golden Gate Park," they have been referred to

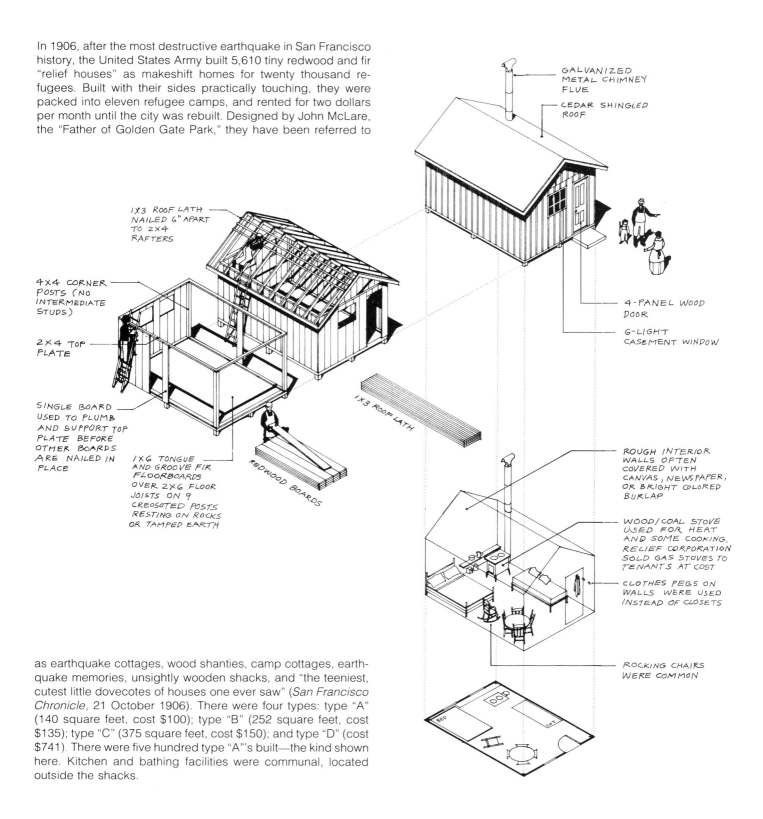

GALVANIZED METAL CHIMNEY FLUE

CEDAR SHINGLED ROOF

1X3 ROOF LATH NAILED 6" APART TO 2X4 RAFTERS

4X4 CORNER POSTS (NO INTERMEDIATE STUDS)

2X4 TOP PLATE

SINGLE BOARD USED TO PLUMB AND SUPPORT TOP PLATE BEFORE OTHER BOARDS ARE NAILED IN PLACE

1X6 TONGUE AND GROOVE FIR FLOORBOARDS OVER 2X6 FLOOR JOISTS ON 9 CREOSOTED POSTS RESTING ON ROCKS OR TAMPED EARTH

1X3 ROOF LATH

REDWOOD BOARDS

4-PANEL WOOD DOOR

6-LIGHT CASEMENT WINDOW

ROUGH INTERIOR WALLS OFTEN COVERED WITH CANVAS, NEWSPAPER, OR BRIGHT COLORED BURLAP

WOOD/COAL STOVE USED FOR HEAT AND SOME COOKING. RELIEF CORPORATION SOLD GAS STOVES TO TENANTS AT COST

CLOTHES PEGS ON WALLS WERE USED INSTEAD OF CLOSETS

ROCKING CHAIRS WERE COMMON

as earthquake cottages, wood shanties, camp cottages, earthquake memories, unsightly wooden shacks, and "the teeniest, cutest little dovecotes of houses one ever saw" (*San Francisco Chronicle*, 21 October 1906). There were four types: type "A" (140 square feet, cost $100); type "B" (252 square feet, cost $135); type "C" (375 square feet, cost $150); and type "D" (cost $741). There were five hundred type "A"'s built—the kind shown here. Kitchen and bathing facilities were communal, located outside the shacks.

Circa 1908   Camp Richmond

Refugee shacks were built in very tight rows and painted olive drab to blend in with the greenery of the site. At one time the shacks held a population of 16,448 people.

Circa 1906   Camp Richmond

Over the years, the shacks have been all but forgotten. What cottages are left are overshadowed by modern developments, wedged between apartment buildings and condominium complexes. Two years ago, however, Jane Cryan, a San Francisco jazz pianist who found herself living in one, started the Society for the Preservation and Appreciation of San Francisco Refugee Shacks. So far they have located only forty-six shacks, but they believe that as many as three hundred might still exist. The society has a band of fifty volunteers that comb the streets to locate other shacks that have survived San Francisco climate and redevelopment.

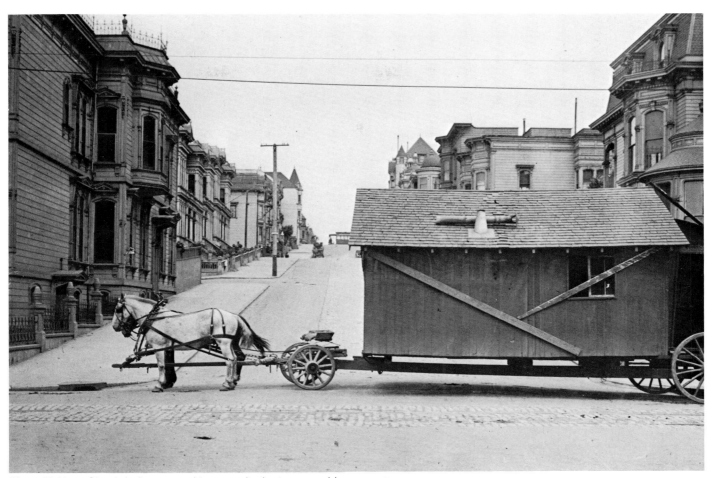

Circa 1910   Shack being moved to new site by team and haywagon

By late 1907, many refugees had been relocated. The shacks were then carted by horse all over the city and converted into rental cottages, garages, storage spaces, or shops.

Circa 1985   Bailey Shack, Telegraph Hill

The type "A" refugee shacks were remarkably well designed considering they cost only one hundred dollars. The quality of their craftsmanship and building technology was such that many have survived and are being lived in today. The Bailey Shack, owned and inhabited by Bill Bailey, is a perfect example. Located next to a huge office building on a tiny plot at the top of Telegraph Hill overlooking the city, it has to be one of San Francisco's most charming homes.

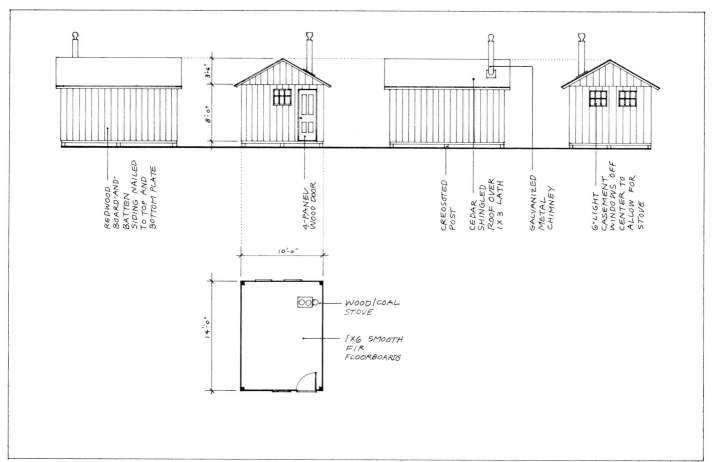

REDWOOD BOARD-AND-BATTEN SIDING NAILED TO TOP AND BOTTOM PLATE

4-PANEL WOOD DOOR

3'-6"

8'-0"

CREOSOTED POST

CEDAR SHINGLED ROOF OVER 1 X 3 LATH

GALVANIZED METAL CHIMNEY

6-LIGHT CASEMENT WINDOWS OFF CENTER TO ALLOW FOR STOVE

10'-0"

14'-0"

WOOD/COAL STOVE

1 X 6 SMOOTH FIR FLOORBOARDS

Plans and Elevations

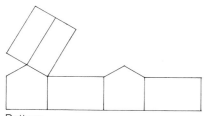

Pattern

The pattern shown here is of the prototypical type "A" refugee shack. There were no side windows because the buildings were located side by side in rows right next to one another. Gentle roof pitch to economize on materials, three small inexpensive windows, door, siding and creosoted-post foundation, were the primary elements of the prototype.

Pink House

27' x 12'
324 square feet

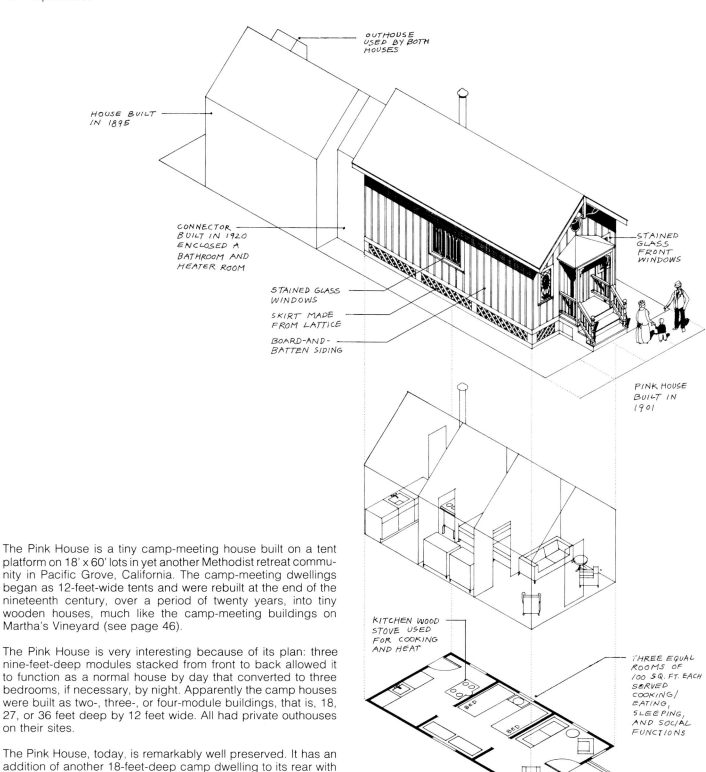

OUTHOUSE USED BY BOTH HOUSES

HOUSE BUILT IN 1895

CONNECTOR BUILT IN 1920 ENCLOSED A BATHROOM AND HEATER ROOM

STAINED GLASS WINDOWS

SKIRT MADE FROM LATTICE

BOARD-AND-BATTEN SIDING

STAINED GLASS FRONT WINDOWS

PINK HOUSE BUILT IN 1901

KITCHEN WOOD STOVE USED FOR COOKING AND HEAT

THREE EQUAL ROOMS OF 100 SQ. FT. EACH SERVED COOKING/ EATING, SLEEPING, AND SOCIAL FUNCTIONS

The Pink House is a tiny camp-meeting house built on a tent platform on 18' x 60' lots in yet another Methodist retreat community in Pacific Grove, California. The camp-meeting dwellings began as 12-feet-wide tents and were rebuilt at the end of the nineteenth century, over a period of twenty years, into tiny wooden houses, much like the camp-meeting buildings on Martha's Vineyard (see page 46).

The Pink House is very interesting because of its plan: three nine-feet-deep modules stacked from front to back allowed it to function as a normal house by day that converted to three bedrooms, if necessary, by night. Apparently the camp houses were built as two-, three-, or four-module buildings, that is, 18, 27, or 36 feet deep by 12 feet wide. All had private outhouses on their sites.

The Pink House, today, is remarkably well preserved. It has an addition of another 18-feet-deep camp dwelling to its rear with a bathroom connector added in 1920.

Board-and-batten siding was commonly used during the Victorian period in America, because it emphasized verticality. The board-and-batten technology used on the Pink House is shown below. The boards are smooth, the battens cut from picture molding, and both are painted semigloss pink.

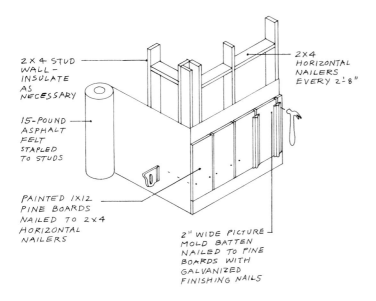

2 X 4 STUD WALL — INSULATE AS NECESSARY

2X4 HORIZONTAL NAILERS EVERY 2'-8"

15-POUND ASPHALT FELT STAPLED TO STUDS

PAINTED 1X12 PINE BOARDS NAILED TO 2X4 HORIZONTAL NAILERS

2" WIDE PICTURE MOLD BATTEN NAILED TO PINE BOARDS WITH GALVANIZED FINISHING NAILS

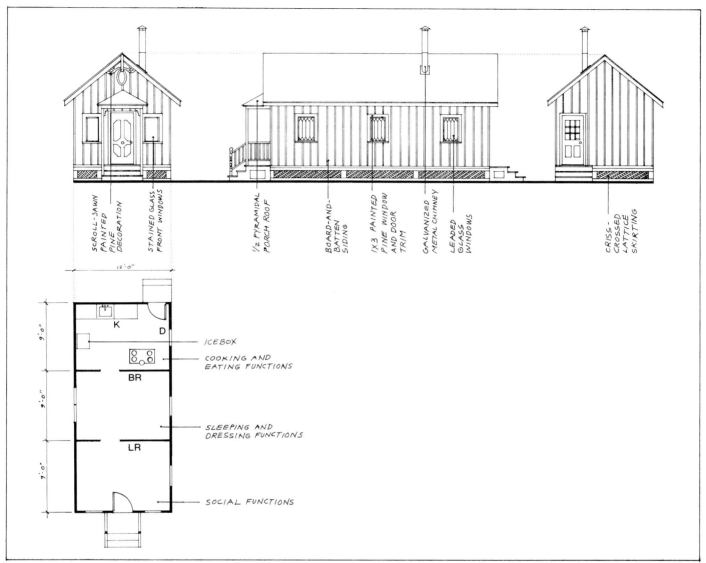

SCROLL-SAWN PAINTED PINE DECORATION

STAINED GLASS FRONT WINDOWS

½ PYRAMIDAL PORCH ROOF

BOARD-AND-BATTEN SIDING

1X3 PAINTED PINE WINDOW AND DOOR TRIM

GALVANIZED METAL CHIMNEY

LEADED GLASS WINDOWS

CRISS-CROSSED LATTICE SKIRTING

12'-0"

9'-0"

9'-0"

9'-0"

K   D

BR

LR

ICEBOX

COOKING AND EATING FUNCTIONS

SLEEPING AND DRESSING FUNCTIONS

SOCIAL FUNCTIONS

Plans and Elevations

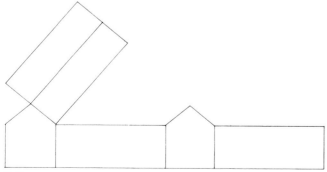

Pattern

The shape of the Pink House is like a long, thin army barracks. Side-yard setbacks were only 3 feet, so each house was only 6 feet from its neighbor. Stained glass was often used in the side windows, which allowed translucent light to enter but prohibited a view directly into the next-door house. These camp-meeting houses were built on platforms raised 18 inches off the ground to allow air to circulate and to control decay.

The Pink House is quite similar to the 1906 San Francisco earthquake refugee shacks (page 69) but maintains a Victorian character with its porches, large windows, elaborate gingerbread trim, and color.

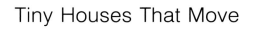
Tiny Houses That Move

Rolling Home

7' x 6'
42 square feet

This tiny rolling home, a remodeled 1949 International delivery van named "Patience," is one of many in a wonderful book called *Rolling Homes: Handmade Houses on Wheels*, by Jane Lidz (see Bibliography). The van shown here was converted into living quarters in 1978 at the cost of $1,500. It is a complete living environment on wheels with sink, shower, toilet, lights,

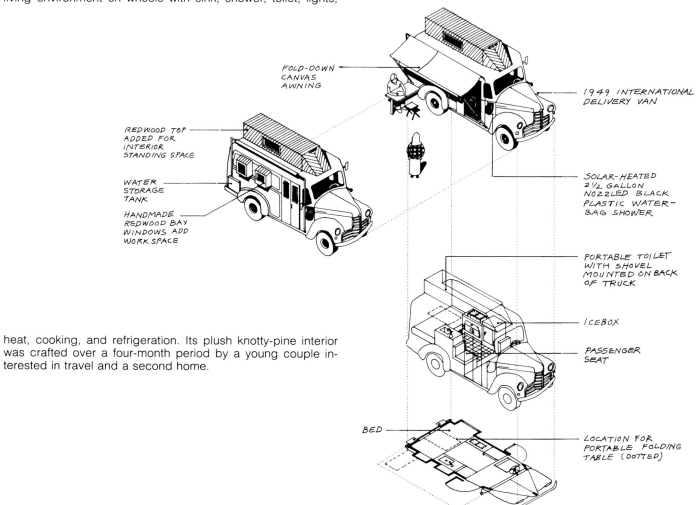

FOLD-DOWN CANVAS AWNING

REDWOOD TOP ADDED FOR INTERIOR STANDING SPACE

WATER STORAGE TANK

HANDMADE REDWOOD BAY WINDOWS ADD WORK SPACE

1949 INTERNATIONAL DELIVERY VAN

SOLAR-HEATED 2½ GALLON NOZZLED BLACK PLASTIC WATER-BAG SHOWER

PORTABLE TOILET WITH SHOVEL MOUNTED ON BACK OF TRUCK

ICEBOX

PASSENGER SEAT

BED

LOCATION FOR PORTABLE FOLDING TABLE (DOTTED)

heat, cooking, and refrigeration. Its plush knotty-pine interior was crafted over a four-month period by a young couple interested in travel and a second home.

The water system begins with a plastic, recreation-vehicle twelve-gallon water storage tank mounted on the exterior of the truck, filled whenever possible. It is painted black so that the water retains solar heat. The water is pumped manually by a combination faucet/pump into a standard porcelain sink. This system can be designed from any recreation-vehicle accessory catalog.

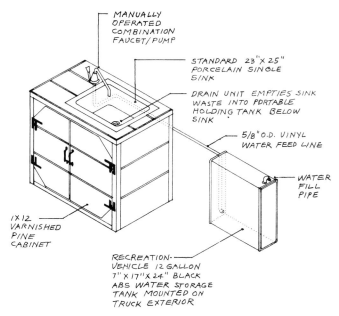

MANUALLY OPERATED COMBINATION FAUCET/PUMP

STANDARD 23"x 25" PORCELAIN SINGLE SINK

DRAIN UNIT EMPTIES SINK WASTE INTO PORTABLE HOLDING TANK BELOW SINK

5/8" O.D. VINYL WATER FEED LINE

WATER FILL PIPE

1X12 VARNISHED PINE CABINET

RECREATION-VEHICLE 12 GALLON 7"X 17"X 24" BLACK ABS WATER STORAGE TANK MOUNTED ON TRUCK EXTERIOR

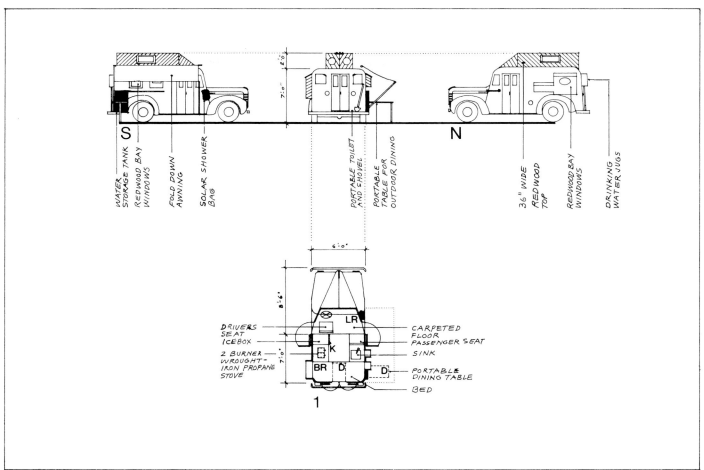

S — WATER STORAGE TANK · REDWOOD BAY WINDOWS · FOLD DOWN AWNING · SOLAR SHOWER BAG · PORTABLE TOILET AND SHOVEL · PORTABLE TABLE FOR OUTDOOR DINING · N · 36" WIDE REDWOOD TOP · REDWOOD BAY WINDOWS · DRINKING WATER JUGS

DRIVERS SEAT
ICEBOX
2 BURNER WROUGHT-IRON PROPANE STOVE

LR
K
BR   D

CARPETED FLOOR
PASSENGER SEAT
SINK
PORTABLE DINING TABLE
D
BED

1

Plans and Elevations

A rooftop, boxlike structure on the exterior of the truck is used to raise the roof level to gain standing room (photograph at the right), and three small boxes added to the sides of the truck provide more interior work space. The inside is wonderfully handcrafted with wood paneling, carpeting, handmade quilts, secondhand windows, and a wide variety of functioning antiques, such as the wrought-iron cookstove, the porcelain sink, and several oil lamps. The ambiance is one of a cozy home—unique when it's inside a delivery van.

Mobile Tool House

10' x 7'
70 square feet

In the summer of 1984, Patrick Green of Temple Hills, Maryland, built this mobile tool house primarily to transport his tools and supplies from one job to another and to provide him with an on-site work space. But the tiny building also serves as a road-side advertisement, speaking well for his craftsmanship, and brings in new business from passersby.

Outside, the small window and dormers provide light to the interior, and create on a tiny scale a houselike workshop that can legally be taken on the road.

Inside there is plenty of light and 24 linear feet of 2-feet-deep bench space. By replacing the benches with beds and adding a small kitchen, perhaps in the space opposite the door, the house would easily convert to a semitransportable dwelling space. Or it could be planned like the tiny raft house (pages 88–89) with its outside kitchen.

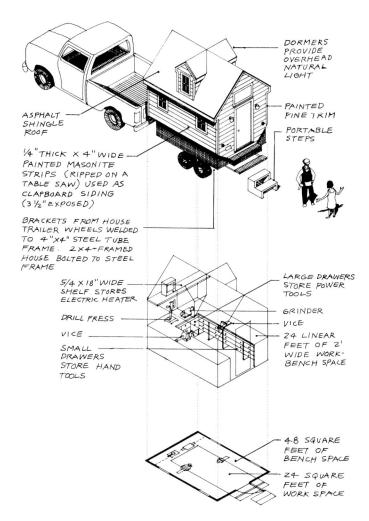

DORMERS PROVIDE OVERHEAD NATURAL LIGHT

PAINTED PINE TRIM

PORTABLE STEPS

ASPHALT SHINGLE ROOF

1/4" THICK X 4" WIDE PAINTED MASONITE STRIPS (RIPPED ON A TABLE SAW) USED AS CLAPBOARD SIDING (3 1/2" EXPOSED)

BRACKETS FROM HOUSE TRAILER WHEELS WELDED TO 4"X4" STEEL TUBE FRAME. 2X4-FRAMED HOUSE BOLTED TO STEEL FRAME

5/4 X 18" WIDE SHELF STORES ELECTRIC HEATER

DRILL PRESS

VICE

SMALL DRAWERS STORE HAND TOOLS

LARGE DRAWERS STORE POWER TOOLS

GRINDER

VICE

24 LINEAR FEET OF 2' WIDE WORK-BENCH SPACE

48 SQUARE FEET OF BENCH SPACE

24 SQUARE FEET OF WORK SPACE

Dormer construction, the key detail to the style of this tiny house, is shown below. The two dormers require a little more framing and finishing time, but they are so small that the job remains interesting throughout.

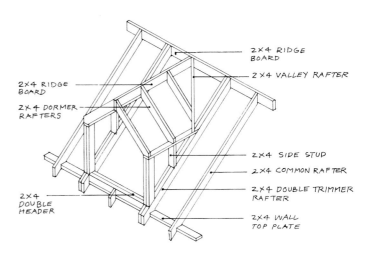

2X4 RIDGE BOARD

2 X4 VALLEY RAFTER

2X4 RIDGE BOARD

2X4 DORMER RAFTERS

2X4 SIDE STUD

2X4 COMMON RAFTER

2X4 DOUBLE TRIMMER RAFTER

2X4 DOUBLE HEADER

2X4 WALL TOP PLATE

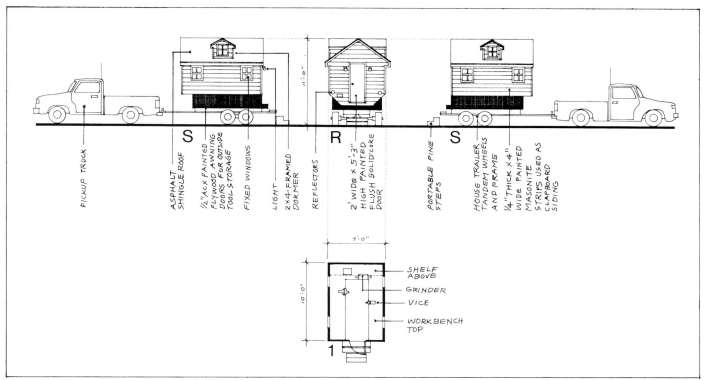

PICKUP TRUCK

ASPHALT SHINGLE ROOF

½"ACX PAINTED PLYWOOD AWNING DOORS FOR OUTSIDE TOOL STORAGE

FIXED WINDOWS

LIGHT

2×4-FRAMED DORMER

REFLECTORS

2' WIDE × 5'-3" HIGH PAINTED FLUSH SOLIDCORE DOOR

PORTABLE PINE STEPS

HOUSE TRAILER TANDEM WHEELS AND FRAME

¼"THICK ×4" WIDE PAINTED MASONITE STRIPS USED AS CLAPBOARD SIDING

S   R   S

7'-0"

10'-0"

SHELF ABOVE
GRINDER
VICE
WORKBENCH TOP

1

Plans and Elevations

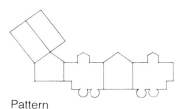

Pattern

The outside siding material is unique. To further reduce the scale, Patrick used ¼" x 4" painted Masonite strips, with 3½" showing. The eye translates these narrow clapboards to the normal ½" x 6" variety—thus the scale reduction. The door is only 5'-3" high, and, again, the eye translates this size to the normal 6'-8" door height. The mobile tool house looks very out of place on the highway, but its purpose is to be eye-catching, and that certainly has been achieved.

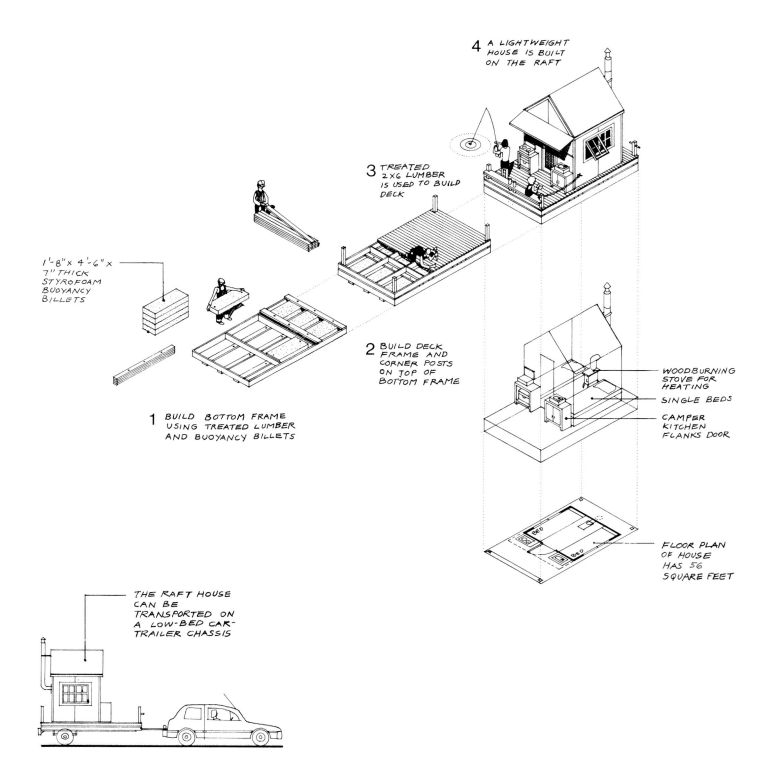

4 A LIGHTWEIGHT HOUSE IS BUILT ON THE RAFT

3 TREATED 2×6 LUMBER IS USED TO BUILD DECK

1'-8" X 4'-6" X 7" THICK STYROFOAM BUOYANCY BILLETS

2 BUILD DECK FRAME AND CORNER POSTS ON TOP OF BOTTOM FRAME

1 BUILD BOTTOM FRAME USING TREATED LUMBER AND BUOYANCY BILLETS

WOODBURNING STOVE FOR HEATING

SINGLE BEDS

CAMPER KITCHEN FLANKS DOOR

FLOOR PLAN OF HOUSE HAS 56 SQUARE FEET

THE RAFT HOUSE CAN BE TRANSPORTED ON A LOW-BED CAR-TRAILER CHASSIS

Raft House

8' x 7' plus deck
56 square feet

The raft house is a tiny houseboat built like the tarpaper house (pages 130–133) on a flat deck supported by buoyancy billets. The house has two single beds and a tiny wood heater. Under an awning outside on the deck is a camper kitchen, and across from it is a bench that can be used for dining or fishing.

The house is designed to be an easy, fast project for houseboat lovers who can't afford a houseboat. The deck is really a dock built with standard marine floating-dock construction methods. The house is built of painted, lightweight ¼" ACX plywood over a frame of 2x3s. It is so small that it can be built by two people in a weekend.

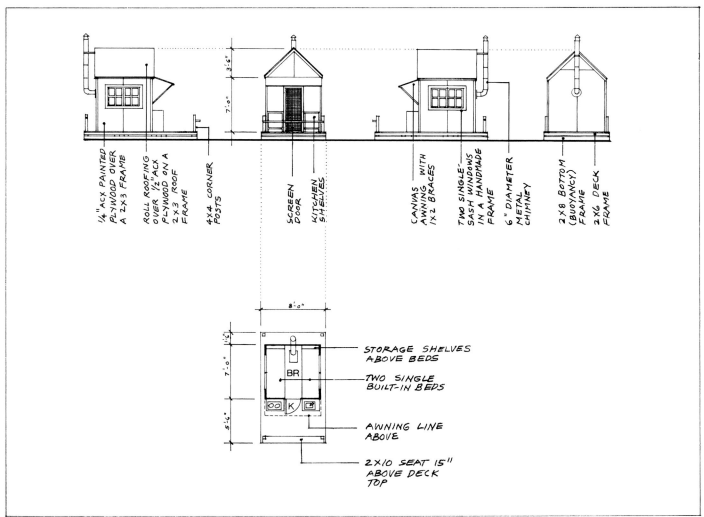

Plans and Elevations

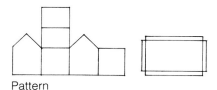

Pattern

Model by Christopher Egan

Portable Shelter Cart

10' x 7'
70 square feet

This wonderful tiny portable, two-person shelter cart was designed in early 1985 by New York architect Christopher Egan, as a proposal to house the urban homeless. It was the most direct of the fifty submissions to a controversial exhibit entitled "The Homeless at Home," shown in New York City at Storefront for Art and Architecture in March 1986.

Christopher Egan defines the urban homeless as "a complex mix including de-institutionalized former patients, displaced workers from failing industries, victims of arson or natural disasters, dropouts, those in desperate need of simple shelter until they can start anew in homes of their own." His shelter carts are to be used in emergencies when the permanent shelters are full. Taken from their storage buildings they would be driven in small caravans to parks, vacant lots, and urban plazas. Some might be clustered in small cart villages around city-owned pavilions that have been converted to clinics or bathhouses where the carts are hooked up to central utilities. Others could be set alone on wide sidewalks, where they rely on their own storage tanks and generators.

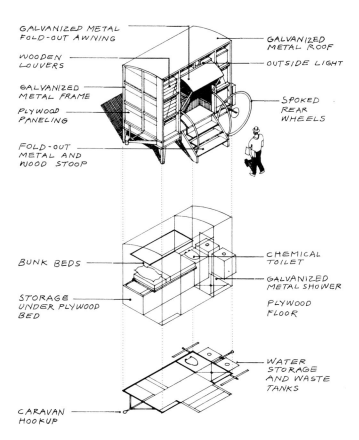

GALVANIZED METAL FOLD-OUT AWNING

WOODEN LOUVERS

GALVANIZED METAL FRAME

PLYWOOD PANELING

FOLD-OUT METAL AND WOOD STOOP

GALVANIZED METAL ROOF

OUTSIDE LIGHT

SPOKED REAR WHEELS

BUNK BEDS

STORAGE UNDER PLYWOOD BED

CHEMICAL TOILET

GALVANIZED METAL SHOWER

PLYWOOD FLOOR

WATER STORAGE AND WASTE TANKS

CARAVAN HOOKUP

Egan describes his design problem as an architectural question: "Assuming a person must live temporarily on the sidewalk, how can we provide shelter that begins to offer the dignity each member of society deserves?" His solution combines the symbols of an urban community (like the wide, steep entry steps, intended to create a personal "stoop") with the minimal function and material requirements of a portable, all-weather shelter. His resulting cart design grows from the basic concerns defined by the homeless themselves: shelter from climate extremes, safe storage of personal belongings, personal hygiene facilities, and privacy.

The Portable Shelter Cart is one way to address a societal problem that demands discussion and a solution. It is included here because it is a tiny home that is a compassionate and thoughtful response to a most difficult and complex dilemma.

Ice Fishing Shanty

7' x 4'-6"
32 square feet

Ice fishing shanties are popular forms of tiny housing in North America wherever there are frozen lakes with fish. Some states, such as Vermont and Minnesota, have wintertime lake villages of thousands of tiny utilitarian buildings, each more special than another.

The basic ice fishing shanty costs about five hundred dollars to build, seats two in a space that contains a kerosene stove, bunks for occasional overnight sleeping, a card table, and

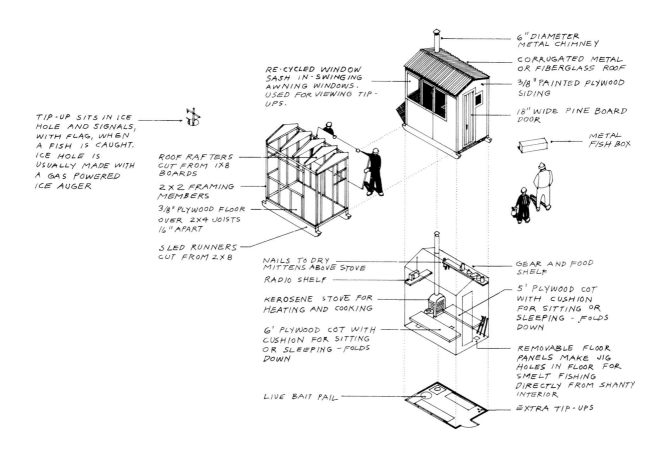

TIP-UP SITS IN ICE HOLE AND SIGNALS, WITH FLAG, WHEN A FISH IS CAUGHT. ICE HOLE IS USUALLY MADE WITH A GAS POWERED ICE AUGER

RE-CYCLED WINDOW SASH IN-SWINGING AWNING WINDOWS. USED FOR VIEWING TIP-UPS.

ROOF RAFTERS CUT FROM 1X8 BOARDS

2 X 2 FRAMING MEMBERS

3/8" PLYWOOD FLOOR OVER 2X4 JOISTS 16" APART

SLED RUNNERS CUT FROM 2X8

NAILS TO DRY MITTENS ABOVE STOVE

RADIO SHELF

KEROSENE STOVE FOR HEATING AND COOKING

6' PLYWOOD COT WITH CUSHION FOR SITTING OR SLEEPING - FOLDS DOWN

LIVE BAIT PAIL

6" DIAMETER METAL CHIMNEY

CORRUGATED METAL OR FIBERGLASS ROOF

3/8" PAINTED PLYWOOD SIDING

18" WIDE PINE BOARD DOOR

METAL FISH BOX

GEAR AND FOOD SHELF

5' PLYWOOD COT WITH CUSHION FOR SITTING OR SLEEPING - FOLDS DOWN

REMOVABLE FLOOR PANELS MAKE JIG HOLES IN FLOOR FOR SMELT FISHING DIRECTLY FROM SHANTY INTERIOR

EXTRA TIP-UPS

shelves for food, utensils, and radio. Fishing is done by viewing outside "tip-ups": a fishing line is placed in a hole drilled in the ice and when a fish takes the bait a flag indicator is tipped up. Sometimes a line is placed directly through a removable panel in the floor of the shanty covering a drilled ice hole, a procedure used for smelt fishing.

Tarpaper

Painted Plywood

Contact paper

Most ice fishing shanties are about 30 square feet and most are the same basic shape. But the materials and craftsmanship used to construct them vary widely. In a village of one or two hundred shanties, there are always twenty or thirty that really catch the eye. These are the ones whose owners are serious do-it-yourselfers and who have set out to build themselves a little masterpiece. The tarpaper house with blue painted lattice battens and translucent fiberglass roof, shown on the upper left hand corner of this page, is such a work of art. The interior is varnished plywood (good side facing in) with blue door and window trim. The roof acts as a greenhouse and the black walls absorb heat from the sun. This shanty, with its attention to detail, is one of the most intelligent tiny houses in the book.

The shanty on the upper right hand corner is included because of its interesting architecture. The small vent over the door and the cantilevered piece containing the heater give it the look of a normal-sized house.

The shanty on the lower left shows how one's imagination can wander when building just for oneself. A translucent roof, pink and yellow floral contact paper (on plywood), siding with red battens, and sliding windows gives a certain identity to this shanty.

Ice fishing shanty villages seem eerily deserted on cold days when everyone is inside fishing. The tiny scale of the buildings and the neatness of the folk architecture create a wonderful kind of anarchistic, unplanned community existing nowhere but on a frozen lake.

Pulling a shanty

Typical interior

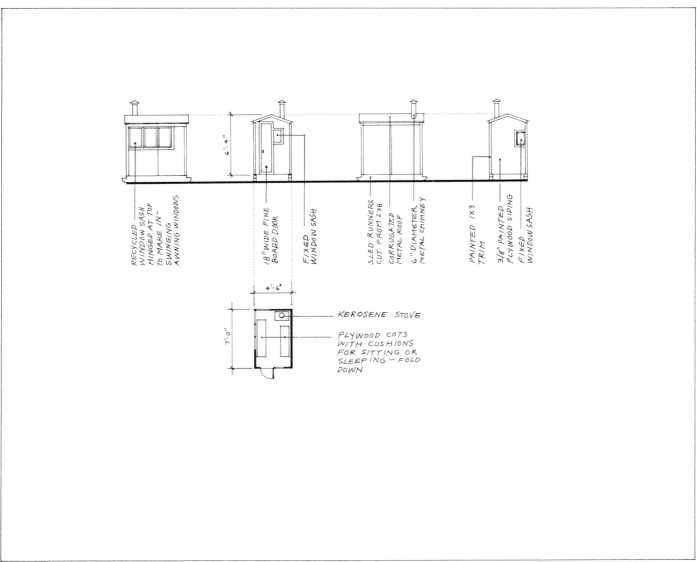

RECYCLED WINDOW SASH HINGED AT TOP TO MAKE IN-SWINGING AWNING WINDOWS

18"WIDE PINE BOARD DOOR

FIXED WINDOW SASH

SLED RUNNERS CUT FROM 2×8

CORRUGATED METAL ROOF

6"DIAMETER, METAL CHIMNEY

PAINTED 1×3 TRIM

3/8" PAINTED PLYWOOD SIDING

FIXED WINDOW SASH

6'-4"

4'-6"

7'-0"

KEROSENE STOVE

PLYWOOD COTS WITH CUSHIONS FOR SITTING OR SLEEPING – FOLD DOWN

Plans and Elevations

Pattern

The ice fishing shanty is built on 2x6 sled runners so that it can be pulled (usually by pickup truck) onto the ice or moved to a better location. When the ice fishing season ends, they are loaded into the pickup and taken home to rest in the backyard until the next winter.

There are two types of ice fishing shanty plans. The one shown above, the most common, has the door set in the front of the gabled end. Another popular plan has the door set in the middle of the side wall (see photo, bottom of page 92). Both plans have strategically placed windows so that the tip-ups can be seen while sitting.

Tiny Prefabricated Houses

Cluster Shed

16' x 12'
192 square feet

Cluster Shed Number One is the smallest of four basic prefabricated Cluster Shed designs, manufactured and shipped by Timberpeg, Inc., of Claremont, New Hampshire, 03743. Double-pane insulated windows, patio doors, hardware, and trim are also included in the package they ship. The owner must provide the foundation with a first-floor platform, interior walls and doors, plumbing, fixtures, kitchen cabinets, and electricity. In other

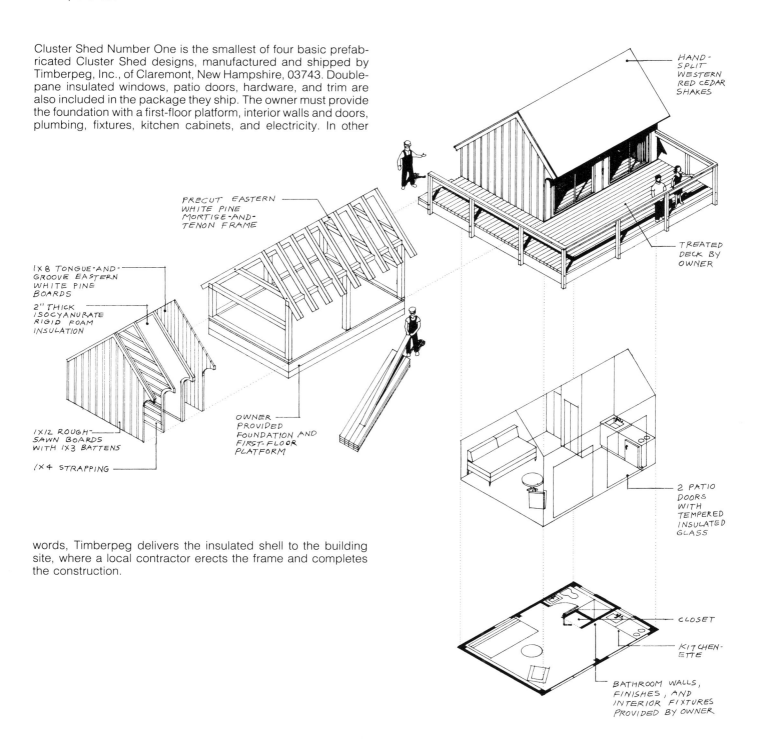

HAND-SPLIT WESTERN RED CEDAR SHAKES

PRECUT EASTERN WHITE PINE MORTISE-AND-TENON FRAME

1X8 TONGUE-AND-GROOVE EASTERN WHITE PINE BOARDS

2" THICK ISOCYANURATE RIGID FOAM INSULATION

1X12 ROUGH-SAWN BOARDS WITH 1X3 BATTENS

1X4 STRAPPING

OWNER PROVIDED FOUNDATION AND FIRST-FLOOR PLATFORM

TREATED DECK BY OWNER

2 PATIO DOORS WITH TEMPERED INSULATED GLASS

CLOSET

KITCHEN-ETTE

BATHROOM WALLS, FINISHES, AND INTERIOR FIXTURES PROVIDED BY OWNER

words, Timberpeg delivers the insulated shell to the building site, where a local contractor erects the frame and completes the construction.

Exposed post-and-beam construction, borrowed from colonial American house- and barn-building technology, is the hallmark of the Cluster Shed design and Timberpeg's unique technology. Oversized, rough-cut eastern white pine members are secured to one another with mortise-and-tenon joints, which are then

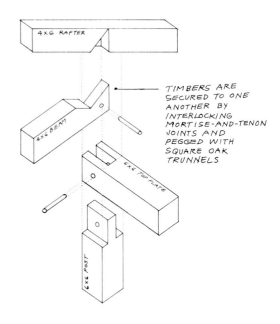

4×6 RAFTER

4×6 BEAM

TIMBERS ARE SECURED TO ONE ANOTHER BY INTERLOCKING MORTISE-AND-TENON JOINTS AND PEGGED WITH SQUARE OAK TRUNNELS

6×6 TOP PLATE

6×6 POST

pegged together with square oak trunnels. The exposed timbers create a handsome, natural interior and a strong frame for the layers of siding, roofing, and insulation.

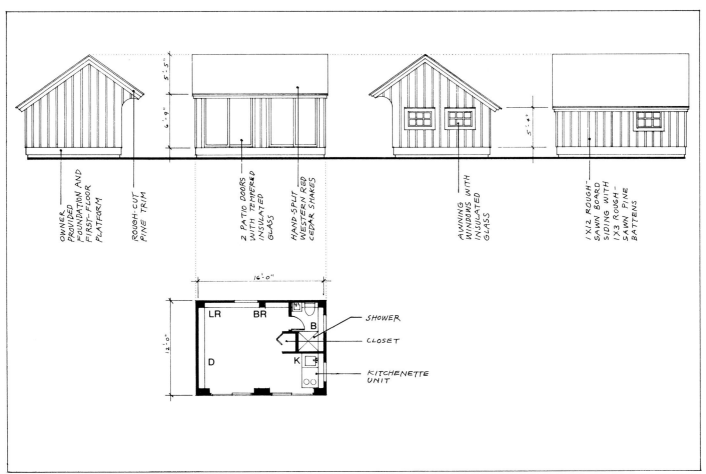

Plans and Elevations

Labels in the elevations/plan:

OWNER PROVIDED FOUNDATION AND FIRST-FLOOR PLATFORM

ROUGH-CUT PINE TRIM

2 PATIO DOORS WITH TEMPERED INSULATED GLASS

HAND-SPLIT WESTERN RED CEDAR SHAKES

AWNING WINDOWS WITH INSULATED GLASS

1X12 ROUGH-SAWN BOARD SIDING WITH 1X3 ROUGH-SAWN PINE BATTENS

5'-5"
6'-9"
5'-4"
16'-0"
12'-0"

LR   BR   B
D   K

SHOWER
CLOSET
KITCHENETTE UNIT

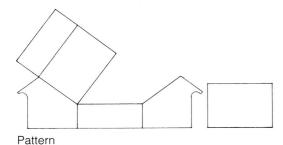

Pattern

The Cluster Shed is designed to be woodsy and rustic inside and out with a style modeled after vernacular shed and barn buildings throughout rural America. All the finish materials are pine and are designed to enhance the style.

Backyard Retreat

8' x 6'
48 square feet

This tiny backyard retreat is made by Walpole Woodworkers (767 East St., Walpole, MA, 02081), a company that specializes in small prefabricated wooden service buildings. Their Building Number One, shown here, makes a wonderful little 6' x 8' retreat that can be erected in a day by two people. The owner simply bolts large panelized sections together, using predrilled holes. Foundation work is minimal and can be done by someone who is reasonably handy.

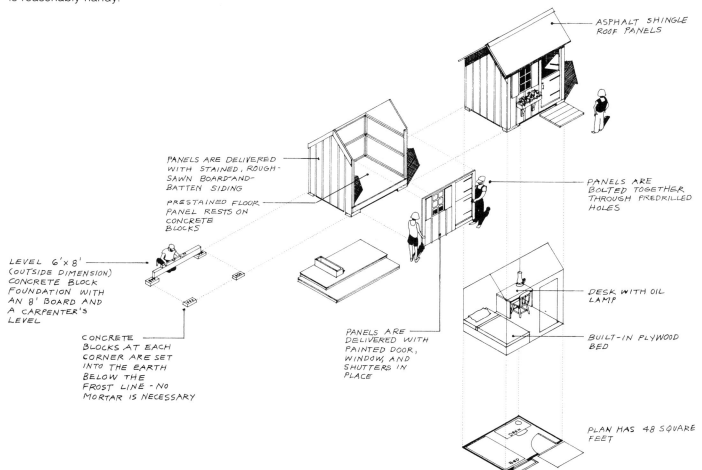

ASPHALT SHINGLE ROOF PANELS

PANELS ARE DELIVERED WITH STAINED, ROUGH-SAWN BOARD-AND-BATTEN SIDING

PRESTAINED FLOOR PANEL RESTS ON CONCRETE BLOCKS

PANELS ARE BOLTED TOGETHER THROUGH PREDRILLED HOLES

LEVEL 6' x 8' (OUTSIDE DIMENSION) CONCRETE BLOCK FOUNDATION WITH AN 8' BOARD AND A CARPENTER'S LEVEL

CONCRETE BLOCKS AT EACH CORNER ARE SET INTO THE EARTH BELOW THE FROST LINE - NO MORTAR IS NECESSARY

PANELS ARE DELIVERED WITH PAINTED DOOR, WINDOW, AND SHUTTERS IN PLACE

DESK WITH OIL LAMP

BUILT-IN PLYWOOD BED

PLAN HAS 48 SQUARE FEET

With the addition of a built-in plywood bed/couch, a desk, and lamp, this little premade utility building can become a George Bernard Shaw writing hut (pages 136–37) or a small guest house (like the one shown on pages 146–49).

Walpole Woodworkers ship a wide variety of wooden backyard buildings ranging from Number One, at 48 square feet, to Number Twenty, their largest, at 200 square feet. They are among the best crafted, best styled garden utility buildings available in this country, and for $1.00 their catalog is a bargain, even if only used for ideas. The possibilities of their buildings are limited only by the owners' imaginations.

The photographs below illustrate how two people can erect the Walpole Woodworkers structure in a very short amount of time. Because the building is shipped to the site completely stained, with doors, windows, and shutters painted and in place, all that remains after leveling a concrete block foundation is bolting the panels together.

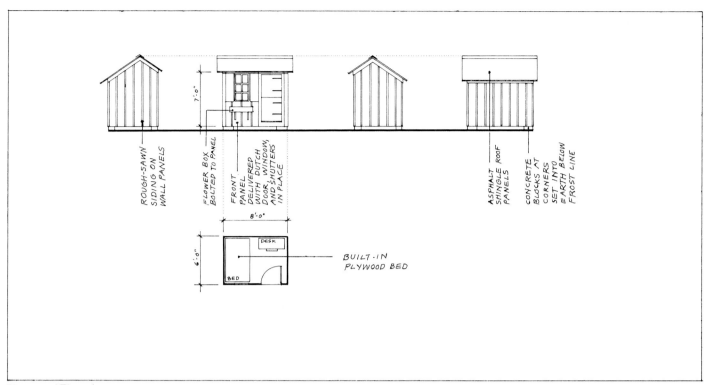

ROUGH-SAWN SIDING ON WALL PANELS

FLOWER BOX BOLTED TO PANEL

FRONT PANEL DELIVERED WITH DUTCH DOOR, WINDOW, AND SHUTTERS IN PLACE

ASPHALT SHINGLE ROOF PANELS

CONCRETE BLOCKS AT CORNERS SET INTO EARTH BELOW FROST LINE

7'-0"

8'-0"

6'-0"

DESK

BED

BUILT-IN PLYWOOD BED

Plans and Elevations

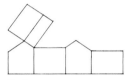

Pattern

The building is styled after American vernacular barn and out-building architecture. It gets a rustic look from its stained rough-sawn boards and battens, and gains its character from bright painted hinged shutters, a flower box, and the Dutch door. The interior consists of smooth vertical pine boards (photograph 2 on preceeding page), which can be stained or painted as the owner wishes.

Rear

Side

Bolt-Together House

8' x 8' plus three 4' x 8' wings plus 4' x 8' sleeping loft
192 square feet

The Bolt-Together House is the first of three prefabricated home structures designed by Jeff Milstein for national magazines (the others are the summer house, pages 112–15, and the tent house, pages 122–25. This one, designed for the March 1972 issue of *Family Circle*, was built in a Connecticut barn and trucked

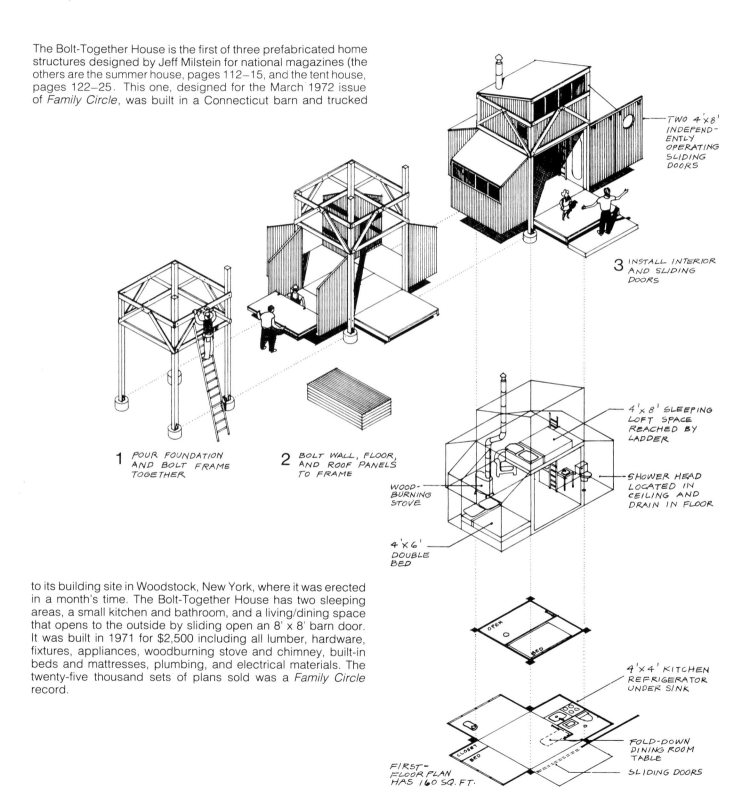

TWO 4'X8' INDEPENDENTLY OPERATING SLIDING DOORS

3 INSTALL INTERIOR AND SLIDING DOORS

4'X8' SLEEPING LOFT SPACE REACHED BY LADDER

SHOWER HEAD LOCATED IN CEILING AND DRAIN IN FLOOR

WOOD-BURNING STOVE

4'X6' DOUBLE BED

1 POUR FOUNDATION AND BOLT FRAME TOGETHER

2 BOLT WALL, FLOOR, AND ROOF PANELS TO FRAME

4'X4' KITCHEN REFRIGERATOR UNDER SINK

FOLD-DOWN DINING ROOM TABLE

SLIDING DOORS

FIRST-FLOOR PLAN HAS 160 SQ. FT.

to its building site in Woodstock, New York, where it was erected in a month's time. The Bolt-Together House has two sleeping areas, a small kitchen and bathroom, and a living/dining space that opens to the outside by sliding open an 8' x 8' barn door. It was built in 1971 for $2,500 including all lumber, hardware, fixtures, appliances, woodburning stove and chimney, built-in beds and mattresses, plumbing, and electrical materials. The twenty-five thousand sets of plans sold was a *Family Circle* record.

Prefabricated, preinsulated plywood sandwich panels are made to bolt to the frame. Window panels are constructed with redwood and Plexiglas and also bolt to the frame.

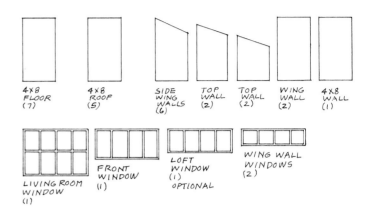

4x8 FLOOR (7)   4x8 ROOF (5)   SIDE WING WALLS (6)   TOP WALL (2)   TOP WALL (2)   WING WALL (2)   4x8 WALL (1)

LIVING ROOM WINDOW (1)   FRONT WINDOW (1)   LOFT WINDOW (1) OPTIONAL   WING WALL WINDOWS (2)

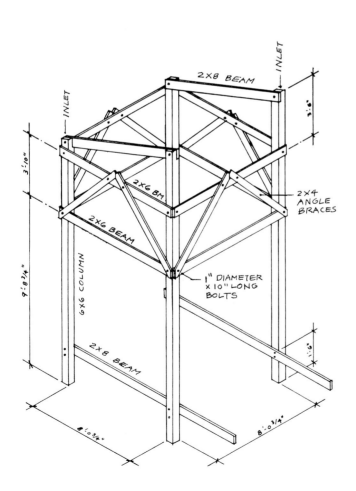

Frame

The frame is made for 6x6 columns with 2x6 and 2x4 braces painted with glossy bright enamel for definition. The panels are engineered to be bolted to the inside of the frame (exposing the frame on the exterior) so that they give rigidity to the structure.

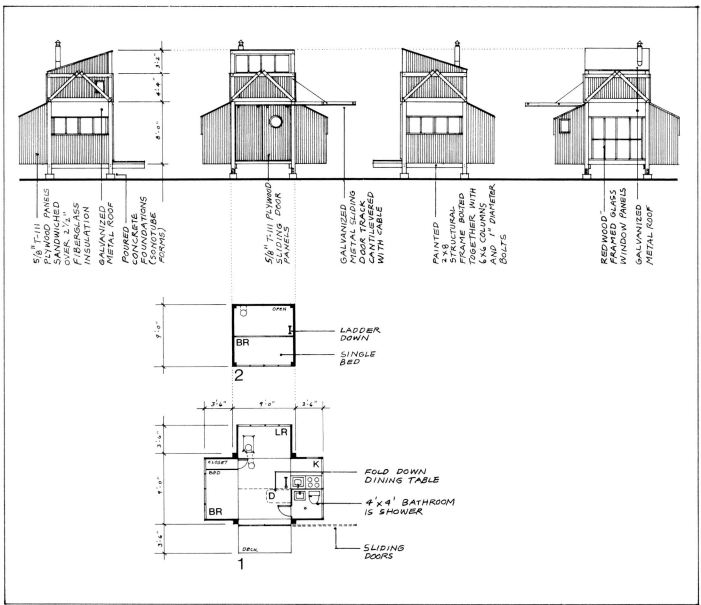

5/8" T-III PLYWOOD PANELS SANDWICHED OVER 2½" FIBERGLASS INSULATION

GALVANIZED METAL ROOF

POURED CONCRETE FOUNDATIONS (SONOTUBE FORMS)

5/8" T-III PLYWOOD SLIDING DOOR PANELS

GALVANIZED METAL SLIDING DOOR TRACK CANTILEVERED WITH CABLE

PAINTED 2×8 STRUCTURAL FRAME BOLTED TOGETHER WITH 6×6 COLUMNS AND 1" DIAMETER BOLTS

REDWOOD FRAMED GLASS WINDOW PANELS

GALVANIZED METAL ROOF

BR

LADDER DOWN

SINGLE BED

2

LR

CLOSET

BED

K

FOLD DOWN DINING TABLE

D

4'×4' BATHROOM IS SHOWER

BR

DECK

SLIDING DOORS

1

Plans and Elevations

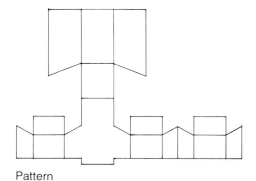

Pattern

Three 4' x 8' cruciform wings (in plan), one containing kitchen and bath, another a bed and closet, and the third the woodstove and living area, all borrow from a central 8' x 8' x 16' high volume. When it is bedtime, the volume serves the bedroom, and when it is daytime, the volume serves the living room.

The exterior is rough-sawn T-111 plywood, and the frame is painted, smooth structural lumber. The roof is of corrugated aluminum. Jeff Milstein grew up and was educated in California. His work is a mixture of the San Francisco Bay Region style (very rustic and, lately, affected by local vernacular barns and sheds) and the high-tech, off-the-shelf, kit-of-parts style espoused by Charles Eames of Los Angeles. The Bolt-Together House is an excellent example of both.

Installing the wall panels

Installing the roof panels

Summer House

10' x 10' plus two sleeping lofts
180 square feet

This panelized summer cottage is another one of Jeff Milstein's kit-of-parts houses, this one designed in 1980 for *Family Circle* magazine as a tiny vacation house for experienced do-it-yourself builders. The house has two little 4'x10' attic sleeping lofts, a bathroom and a kitchen sharing a tiny sink strategically placed under the ladder to the loft, and a common living/dining space with front porch.

3 STRETCH 4-MIL VINYL OVER WINDOWS, NAIL 1X2 BATTENS, BUILD LOFT BEDS AND DECK, AND FINISH OTHER DETAILS

1 BUILD FOUNDATION FRAME AND PLACE FLOOR PANELS

2 ERECT WALL AND ROOF PANELS

4' X 10' LOFT BEDS REACHED BY SHIPS LADDER

PORTABLE TOILET IN 3' X 2' ROOM

BUILT-IN COUCH

BATH/KITCHEN SINK UNDER SHIPS LADDER

As shown in the photograph on the left, prefabricated wall and roof panels are transported to the building site and erected on a 10'x10' deck, which, in turn, rests on four treated posts set below the frost line. The house was designed with economy in mind. For example, the windows are made from stretched clear plastic, the wall panels from 2x3 studs, the siding is 1/2" CDX plywood, the roof is roll roofing, and the kitchen and bathroom are designed with off-the-shelf camper equipment and hardware, requiring no plumbing or electricity.

Though compact, the large windows facing a view of the sky, and the open slot between the lofts to the roof create a spacious feeling. It can be panelized as shown or built with standard platform-frame construction methods with 2x3 stud walls.

The panels, illustrated below, are made with 1/2" CDX plywood and 2x3 studs every 2'-0" on center. Later, after the panels are erected, outside battens are added, 1'-0" on center, and two coats of exterior paint are applied. The panels are uninsulated, but rigid insulation could be installed between the studs and another layer of protective plywood or gypsum board applied as an interior finish.

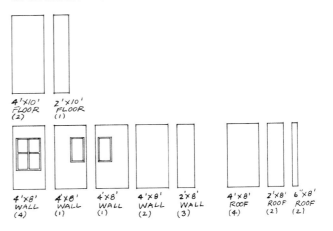

4'x10'
FLOOR
(2)

2'x10'
FLOOR
(1)

4'x8'
WALL
(4)

4'x8'
WALL
(1)

4'x8'
WALL
(1)

4'x8'
WALL
(2)

2'x8'
WALL
(3)

4'x8'
ROOF
(4)

2'x8'
ROOF
(2)

6"x8'
ROOF
(2)

Kitchen

The shared kitchen/bathroom sink and camper water-supply system is beautifully designed below the ladder in a place that would normally be wasted. A small three foot by four foot room adjacent to the ladder contains a portable toilet. The drawing below shows how various catalog-ordered parts are used to create what is normally the most difficult and expensive part of any house to construct.

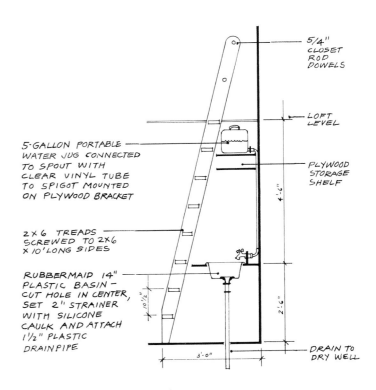

5/4"
CLOSET
ROD
DOWELS

LOFT
LEVEL

5-GALLON PORTABLE
WATER JUG CONNECTED
TO SPOUT WITH
CLEAR VINYL TUBE
TO SPIGOT MOUNTED
ON PLYWOOD BRACKET

PLYWOOD
STORAGE
SHELF

4'-6"

2X6 TREADS
SCREWED TO 2X6
X 10'LONG SIDES

RUBBERMAID 14"
PLASTIC BASIN -
CUT HOLE IN CENTER,
SET 2" STRAINER
WITH SILICONE
CAULK AND ATTACH
1 1/2" PLASTIC
DRAINPIPE

10 1/2"

2'-6"

3'-0"

DRAIN TO
DRY WELL

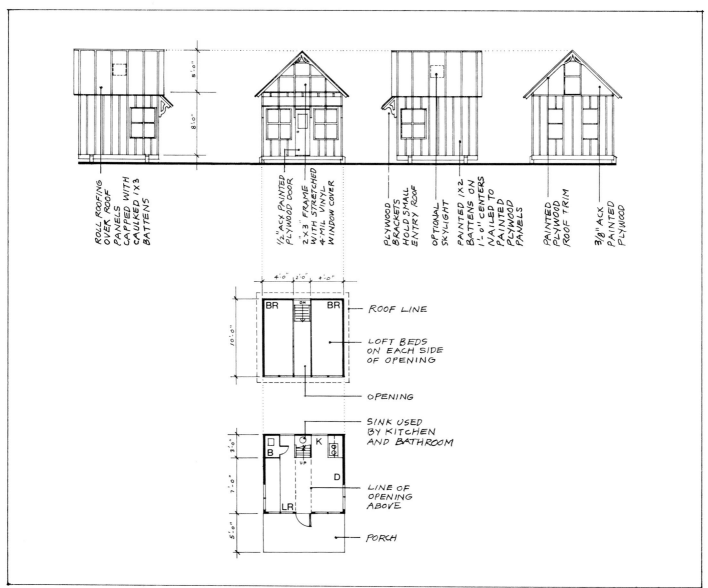

ROLL ROOFING OVER ROOF PANELS CAPPED WITH CAULKED 1×3 BATTENS

1/2"ACX PAINTED PLYWOOD DOOR

2"×3" FRAME WITH STRETCHED 4-MIL VINYL WINDOW COVER

PLYWOOD BRACKETS HOLD SMALL ENTRY ROOF

OPTIONAL SKYLIGHT

PAINTED 1×2 BATTENS ON 1'-0" CENTERS NAILED TO PAINTED PLYWOOD PANELS

PAINTED PLYWOOD ROOF TRIM

3/8" ACX PAINTED PLYWOOD

ROOF LINE

LOFT BEDS ON EACH SIDE OF OPENING

OPENING

SINK USED BY KITCHEN AND BATHROOM

LINE OF OPENING ABOVE

PORCH

Plans and Elevations

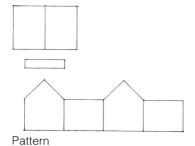

Pattern

Porch roof brackets

The summer house makes an interesting comparison with the Texas Sunday House. Both have attic sleeping, both are one room in size, both have a small front porch, and both have a bit of Carpenter Gothic trim. But the summer house, while smaller, has inside bathroom and kitchen facilities. It would be interesting to bring back some of those turn-of-the century Texas churchgoers to show them the camper equipment technology that is at the heart of this tiny house.

Interchanging panels

Cube House

8'-4" x 8'-4"
69 square feet

The panelized Cube House was designed by myself for *Popular Science* magazine as a little sleeping and studying retreat that could adapt to the changes in the seasons.

The 8' x 8' x 8' frame has two stationary floor and roof panels. A wide variety of wall panels, made to suit the owner's needs

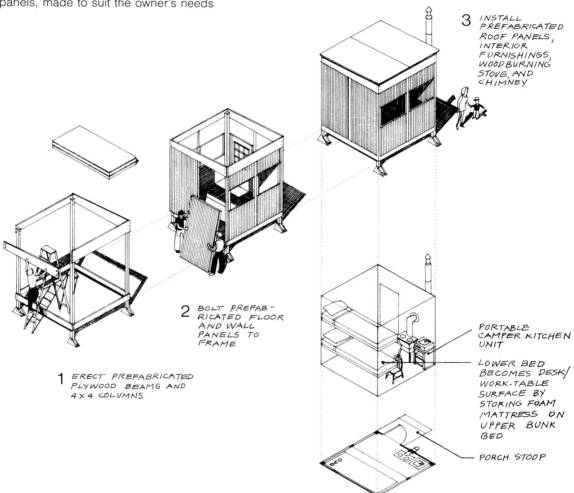

3 INSTALL PREFABRICATED ROOF PANELS, INTERIOR FURNISHINGS, WOODBURNING STOVE, AND CHIMNEY

2 BOLT PREFABRICATED FLOOR AND WALL PANELS TO FRAME

1 ERECT PREFABRICATED PLYWOOD BEAMS AND 4 X 4 COLUMNS

PORTABLE CAMPER KITCHEN UNIT

LOWER BED BECOMES DESK/ WORK-TABLE SURFACE BY STORING FOAM MATTRESS ON UPPER BUNK BED

PORCH STOOP

and site conditions, are interchangeable. With two hours of work, the house can be transformed from a winterized heated little cabin to an open, screened sleeping porch. Complete construction drawings and a materials list were published in the July 1974 issue of *Popular Science*.

The Cube House is designed as a kit-of-parts to be prefabricated at home. It can be shipped flat on a small rented trailer or pickup truck to any site, where it can be bolted together by two people in one day. It is furnished with a small potbelly stove for heat and cooking, a Porta-sink, a camper ice cooler, a small chemical toilet, and two built-in beds.

Two 4' x 8' modular roof and floor panels are necessary. At least eight of the 4' x 8' wall panels (including one door panel) must be chosen and fabricated. The Cube House shown in the photographs has two solid panels, one door panel, three window panels, and two fixed-glass panels. Four supplemental screen panels are installed, front and back, in the Spring, to convert it into a screen house.

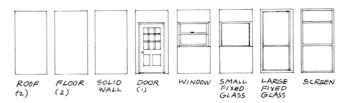

ROOF (2)   FLOOR (2)   SOLID WALL   DOOR (1)   WINDOW   SMALL FIXED GLASS   LARGE FIXED GLASS   SCREEN

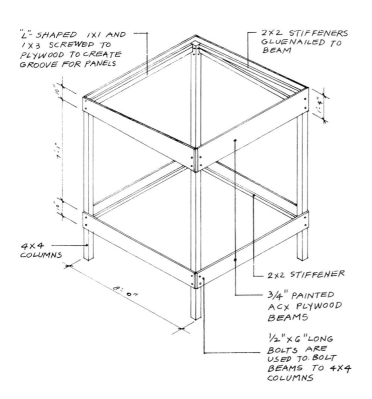

"L" SHAPED 1X1 AND 1X3 SCREWED TO PLYWOOD TO CREATE GROOVE FOR PANELS

2X2 STIFFENERS GLUENAILED TO BEAM

4X4 COLUMNS

2X2 STIFFENER

3/4" PAINTED ACX PLYWOOD BEAMS

1/2" X 6" LONG BOLTS ARE USED TO BOLT BEAMS TO 4X4 COLUMNS

The frame is constructed with 4x4 posts and ¾" plywood beams with 2x2 stiffeners fabricated and prepainted in the shop. Once leveled, it bolts together like an Erector Set and becomes rigid when the roof and floor panels are dropped in place.

The smallest kitchen in the book is made from catalog-ordered camper appliances and a small two-burner woodstove. This kitchen is meant to serve one or two people for a day or two at the most, with drinks and snacks, perhaps a breakfast and a lunch. The tiny cabinet is on casters so that it can be moved away from the stove when wood is burning.

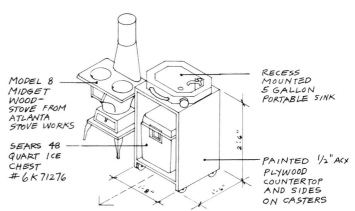

MODEL 8 MIDGET WOOD-STOVE FROM ATLANTA STOVE WORKS

SEARS 48 QUART ICE CHEST #6K71276

RECESS MOUNTED 5 GALLON PORTABLE SINK

PAINTED ½" ACX PLYWOOD COUNTERTOP AND SIDES ON CASTERS

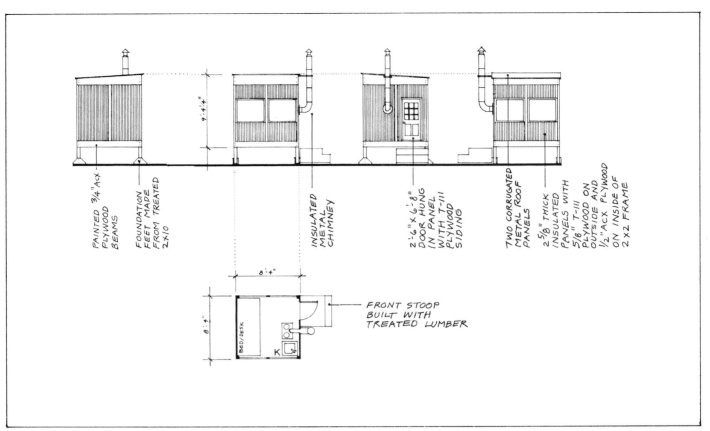

PAINTED ¾" ACX PLYWOOD BEAMS

FOUNDATION FEET MADE FROM TREATED 2×10

INSULATED METAL CHIMNEY

2'-6" × 6'-8" DOOR HUNG IN PANEL WITH T-111 PLYWOOD SIDING

TWO CORRUGATED METAL ROOF PANELS

2⅝" THICK INSULATED PANELS WITH ⅝" T-111 PLYWOOD ON OUTSIDE AND ½" ACX PLYWOOD ON INSIDE OF 2×2 FRAME

8'-4"

8'-4"

BED/DESK

K

FRONT STOOP BUILT WITH TREATED LUMBER

Plans and Elevations

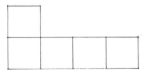

Pattern

The Cube House has been given a woodsy, rustic style with its use of rough-textured, unpainted T-111 plywood as siding for the wall panels. The frame is painted gloss yellow to give it a separate toylike identity and to give the structure a touch of color.

Frame

Tiny Paper and Cloth Houses

Open

Closed

Tent House

11' x 8'
88 square feet

The Tent House is an ingenious tiny house idea conceived and built by New York architect Jeff Milstein for *Popular Science* magazine, using the lightweight, cost-effective advantages of nylon to create space, and protecting it with a small plywood box into which the nylon folds when the house is not in use.

The Tent House, like other Milstein designs shown in this book, is a kit of homemade parts, built in the shop, transported to a site, and erected there, much like an Erector Set. First the 4' x 8' x 8'-high box is bolted together, then a platform is folded down to support the fold-out nylon tent structure. The box contains a camper-style bathroom and kitchen and fold-out Murphy-type bunk beds. The nylon-covered space is used for dining and living by day and for bedroom by night.

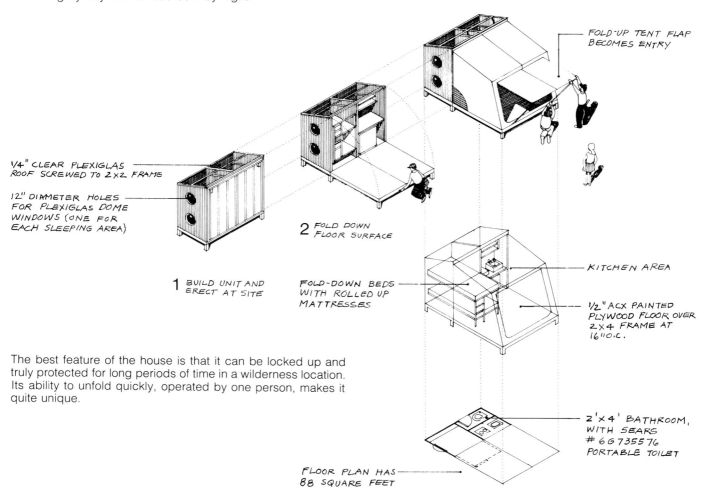

3 ATTACH NYLON TENT

FOLD-UP TENT FLAP BECOMES ENTRY

1/4" CLEAR PLEXIGLAS ROOF SCREWED TO 2x2 FRAME

12" DIAMETER HOLES FOR PLEXIGLAS DOME WINDOWS (ONE FOR EACH SLEEPING AREA)

2 FOLD DOWN FLOOR SURFACE

1 BUILD UNIT AND ERECT AT SITE

FOLD-DOWN BEDS WITH ROLLED UP MATTRESSES

KITCHEN AREA

1/2" ACX PAINTED PLYWOOD FLOOR OVER 2x4 FRAME AT 16" O.C.

The best feature of the house is that it can be locked up and truly protected for long periods of time in a wilderness location. Its ability to unfold quickly, operated by one person, makes it quite unique.

2' x 4' BATHROOM, WITH SEARS # 6G735576 PORTABLE TOILET

FLOOR PLAN HAS 88 SQUARE FEET

Parts

The first step in the building of the Tent House is to fabricate the parts in a comfortable place, such as a basement or garage shop. Next the parts must be transported to a site: the Tent House will fit easily in a small half-ton pickup truck or rented van.

Erection at the site should take two people about one day. Once the camper appliances are set up and a suitable water supply is found, housekeeping can begin.

Folding the beds down

The Tent House kitchen and bath are organized in an amazingly small 4' x 4' space. The kitchen, shown below, is made from painted ½" plywood, and the appliances are ordered from a Sears or other camper equipment catalog. The kitchen occupies slightly less than half of the 4' x 4' space.

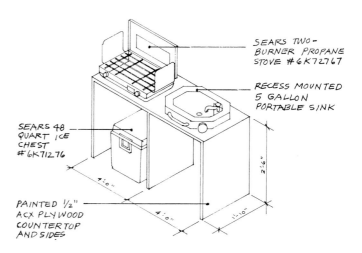

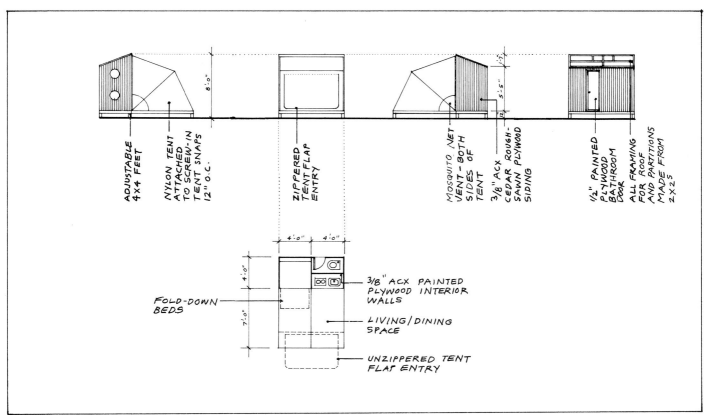

ADJUSTABLE 4X4 FEET

NYLON TENT ATTACHED TO SCREW-IN TENT SNAPS 12" O.C.

ZIPPERED TENT FLAP ENTRY

MOSQUITO NET VENT - BOTH SIDES OF TENT

3/8" ACX CEDAR ROUGH-SAWN PLYWOOD SIDING

1/2" PAINTED PLYWOOD BATHROOM DOOR

ALL FRAMING FOR ROOF AND PARTITIONS MADE FROM 2X2s

FOLD-DOWN BEDS

3/8" ACX PAINTED PLYWOOD INTERIOR WALLS

LIVING/DINING SPACE

UNZIPPERED TENT FLAP ENTRY

Plans and Elevations

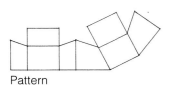

Pattern

Except for the nylon tent cover, the materials for the Tent House can all be purchased from a local lumberyard or home center. Construction methods are all standard, bolt-together techniques, with the exception of the sewing of the nylon. The cover can be made on a home sewing machine using standard sewing techniques. Painting some of the parts gives it a toylike quality, desired by most who inhabit this tiny unfoldable house.

Unzipping the entry

Canvas House

15'-9" x 15'-9"
248 square feet

Maho Bay, a new camping resort on St. John in the U.S. Virgin Islands, is a wonderful community of canvas-wrapped wood-framed cottages linked together by a network of wooden walkways designed by architect James Hadley. The basic structure of both the cottages and the walkways is that of stilt-supported decks, elevated so as not to disturb vulnerable vegetation. The cottages are made of precut hemmed canvas and mosquito netting pieces stapled in an overlapping fashion to a simple wood frame, so they won't leak.

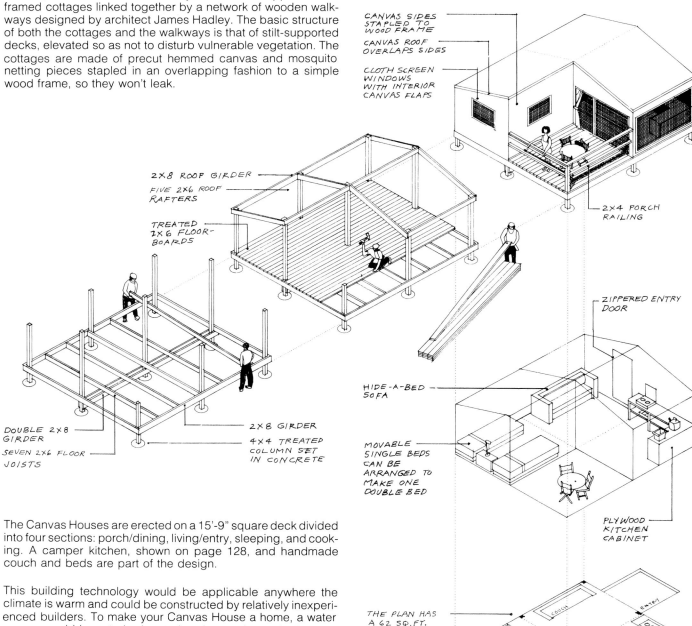

CANVAS SIDES STAPLED TO WOOD FRAME

CANVAS ROOF OVERLAPS SIDES

CLOTH SCREEN WINDOWS WITH INTERIOR CANVAS FLAPS

2X4 PORCH RAILING

2X8 ROOF GIRDER

FIVE 2X6 ROOF RAFTERS

TREATED 2X6 FLOOR-BOARDS

ZIPPERED ENTRY DOOR

DOUBLE 2X8 GIRDER

SEVEN 2X6 FLOOR JOISTS

2X8 GIRDER

4X4 TREATED COLUMN SET IN CONCRETE

HIDE-A-BED SOFA

MOVABLE SINGLE BEDS CAN BE ARRANGED TO MAKE ONE DOUBLE BED

PLYWOOD KITCHEN CABINET

THE PLAN HAS A 62 SQ.FT. BEDROOM, A 62 SQ.FT. LIVING ROOM, A 62 SQ.FT. KITCHEN, AND A 62 SQ.FT. DINING PORCH

The Canvas Houses are erected on a 15'-9" square deck divided into four sections: porch/dining, living/entry, sleeping, and cooking. A camper kitchen, shown on page 128, and handmade couch and beds are part of the design.

This building technology would be applicable anywhere the climate is warm and could be constructed by relatively inexperienced builders. To make your Canvas House a home, a water source would have to be located and an outhouse built.

The time-consuming part of the project is prefabricating the canvas pieces, shown below. An industrial sewing machine is necessary to work with the thick canvas, and some degree of sewing skill is needed. Nylon may be substituted for the canvas but will be less durable.

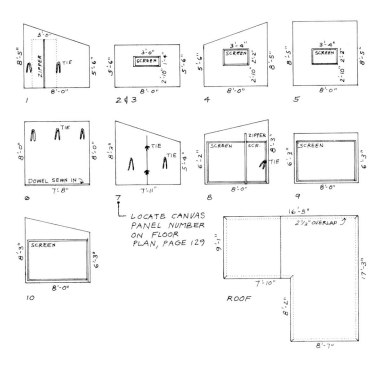

The kitchen is another prefabrication job involving painted ½" plywood and camper equipment ordered from a catalog. The kitchen should be made in pieces, transported flat to the building site, and screwed together there.

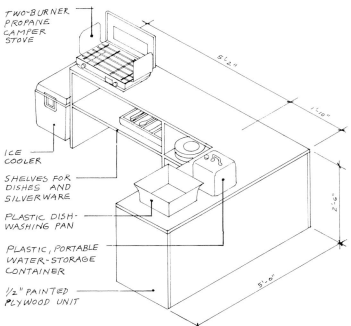

TWO-BURNER
PROPANE
CAMPER
STOVE

ICE
COOLER

SHELVES FOR
DISHES AND
SILVERWARE

PLASTIC DISH-
WASHING PAN

PLASTIC, PORTABLE
WATER-STORAGE
CONTAINER

½" PAINTED
PLYWOOD UNIT

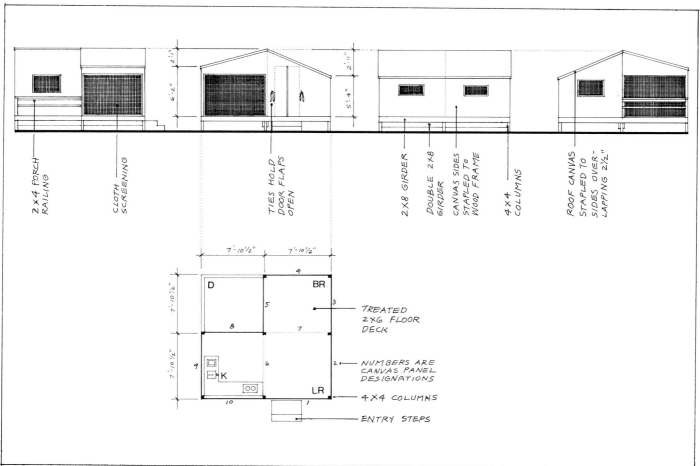

Plans and Elevations

Labels on elevation drawing:
- 2 X 4 PORCH RAILING
- CLOTH SCREENING
- TIES HOLD DOOR FLAPS OPEN
- 2 X 8 GIRDER
- DOUBLE 2 X 8 GIRDER
- CANVAS SIDES STAPLED TO WOOD FRAME
- 4 X 4 COLUMNS
- ROOF CANVAS STAPLED TO SIDES OVER-LAPPING 2½"

Plan labels:
- 7'-10½" 7'-10½"
- 7'-10½" 7'-10½"
- D
- BR
- K
- LR
- TREATED 2 X 6 FLOOR DECK
- NUMBERS ARE CANVAS PANEL DESIGNATIONS
- 4 X 4 COLUMNS
- ENTRY STEPS

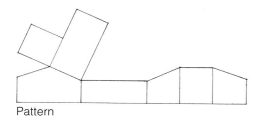

Pattern

Installing the canvas

The frame and deck can be erected in two days by two people. The canvas or nylon pieces can be stapled to the frame (roof last) in another day's work. The end result is an amazingly comfortable cabin with excellent air circulation and a beautiful sound when it rains. The vulnerable canvas or nylon top and sides can, of course, be removed (with some tedious work) and stored for use another time.

Tarpaper House

12' x 8'
96 square feet

By far, the least expensive method of siding a house is to use tar-impregnated building felt-tar paper. This type of cladding is usually viewed as an interim technology, used to protect the building until enough money is raised to install a more proper siding material over the tarpaper. However, as shown here and on the ice-fishing shanty on page 93, tarpaper can be an effective and somewhat pleasing finish material. Its life-span is

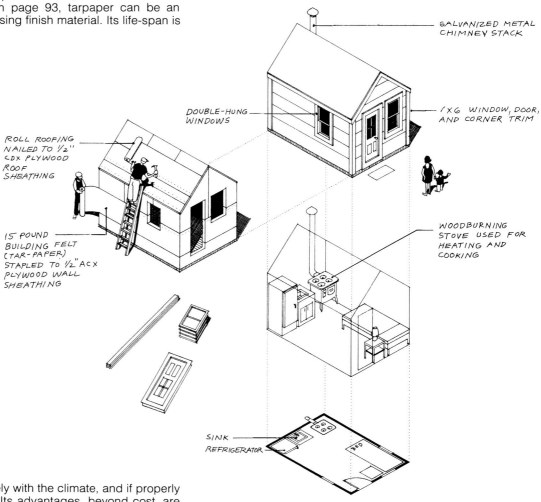

GALVANIZED METAL CHIMNEY STACK

DOUBLE-HUNG WINDOWS

1 X 6 WINDOW, DOOR, AND CORNER TRIM

ROLL ROOFING NAILED TO 1/2" CDX PLYWOOD ROOF SHEATHING

15 POUND BUILDING FELT (TAR-PAPER) STAPLED TO 1/2" ACX PLYWOOD WALL SHEATHING

WOODBURNING STOVE USED FOR HEATING AND COOKING

SINK

REFRIGERATOR

about six years, varying widely with the climate, and if properly battened, it can last longer. Its advantages, beyond cost, are easy installation (staple gun) and heat absorption (the black color will gain heat from the sun).

The house shown here is a tiny getaway cabin in the backyard of a Maine home. It is a complete, functioning tiny building with an outhouse (not shown). It can be built for around $600 using standard construction methods.

As shown below, the tarpaper-sided house is easy to build. The 15-pound saturated building felt is stapled to plywood sheathing and further held in place with wood battens—in this case the painted trim boards.

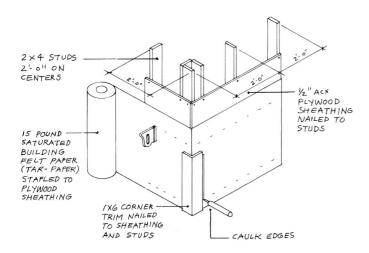

2 X 4 STUDS 2'-0" ON CENTERS

15 POUND SATURATED BUILDING FELT PAPER (TAR- PAPER) STAPLED TO PLYWOOD SHEATHING

1X6 CORNER TRIM NAILED TO SHEATHING AND STUDS

½" ACX PLYWOOD SHEATHING NAILED TO STUDS

CAULK EDGES

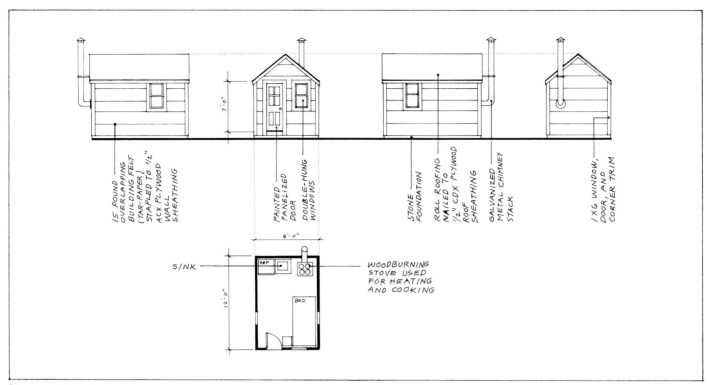

Plans and Elevations

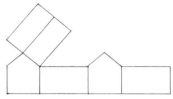

Pattern

Important building materials other than tarpaper are the roll roofing—a self-sealing roll-on asphalt roof material—and the standard double-hung windows and doors. The painted 1x6 pine trim acts as battens for the tarpaper and as crisp finish material to enhance the rough quality of the tarpaper.

Tiny Special-Use Houses

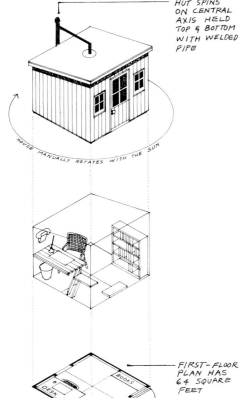

HUT SPINS
ON CENTRAL
AXIS HELD
TOP & BOTTOM
WITH WELDED
PIPE

HOUSE MANUALLY ROTATES WITH THE SUN

FIRST-FLOOR
PLAN HAS
64 SQUARE
FEET

DESK   BOOKS   SHELF

George Bernard Shaw's Writing Hut

8' x 8'
64 square feet

George Bernard Shaw, perhaps the most significant British playwright since the seventeenth century, wrote his most creative work, including his plays *Pygmalion, Heartbreak House, Back to Methuselah,* and *Saint Joan,* in a little writing hut at the bottom of his garden at his home in England.

Shaw designed the hut himself as a tiny office built on a central steel-pole frame so that it could be manually rotated to follow the arc of the sun. He worked alone and loved his privacy; he even adjusted his telephone for outgoing calls only.

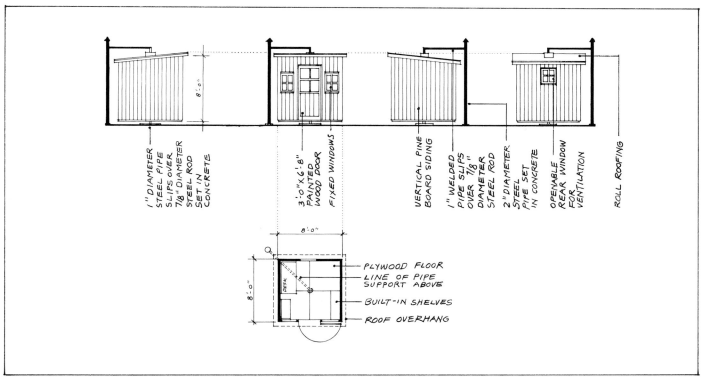

1" DIAMETER STEEL PIPE SLIPS OVER 7/8" DIAMETER STEEL ROD SET IN CONCRETE

3'-0"x6'-8" PAINTED WOOD DOOR

FIXED WINDOWS

VERTICAL PINE BOARD SIDING

1" WELDED PIPE SLIPS OVER 7/8" DIAMETER STEEL ROD

2" DIAMETER STEEL PIPE SET IN CONCRETE

OPENABLE REAR WINDOW FOR VENTILATION

ROLL ROOFING

8'-0"

DESK

PLYWOOD FLOOR
LINE OF PIPE SUPPORT ABOVE
BUILT-IN SHELVES
ROOF OVERHANG

Plans and Elevations

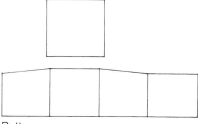

Pattern

Materials used for this small hut are 2x3 frame, rough-cut weathered pine siding, four secondhand windows, roll roofing, and a simple built-in desk and shelves. The interior is the uninsulated, exposed frame and cladding, simply painted.

Picnic House

15' x 15'
219 square feet

Designed by Michael Jantzen in 1976, this modern building sleeps eight and provides them with cooking and dining facilities on a small but expandable central cabinet. The building is designed for warm-weather camping, picnicking, partying, or sleep-outs for one or groups of two to eight. Large hooded areas of screening, installed in the walls, provide ventilation, and a huge plastic domed skylight in the center of the roof illuminates the interior. An optional exterior deck of any size can be constructed facing the best view (a 6-foot-wide L-shape is shown here).

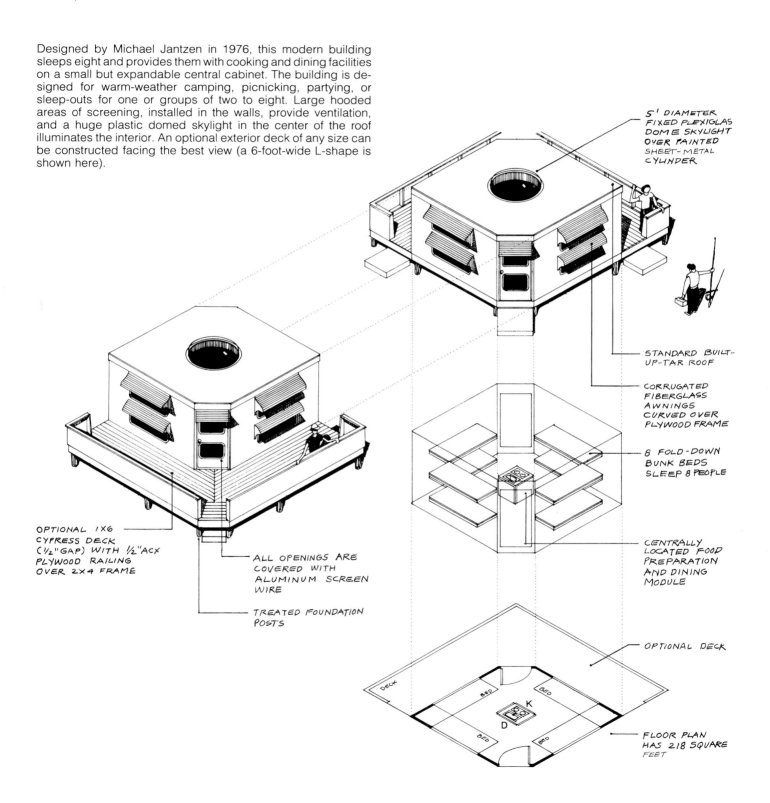

5' DIAMETER FIXED PLEXIGLAS DOME SKYLIGHT OVER PAINTED SHEET-METAL CYLINDER

STANDARD BUILT-UP-TAR ROOF

CORRUGATED FIBERGLASS AWNINGS CURVED OVER PLYWOOD FRAME

8 FOLD-DOWN BUNK BEDS SLEEP 8 PEOPLE

CENTRALLY LOCATED FOOD PREPARATION AND DINING MODULE

OPTIONAL DECK

FLOOR PLAN HAS 218 SQUARE FEET

OPTIONAL 1X6 CYPRESS DECK (1/2" GAP) WITH 1/2" ACX PLYWOOD RAILING OVER 2X4 FRAME

ALL OPENINGS ARE COVERED WITH ALUMINUM SCREEN WIRE

TREATED FOUNDATION POSTS

The wall section, shown below, describes the construction and shows how the beds fold up to provide open space for dance or work.

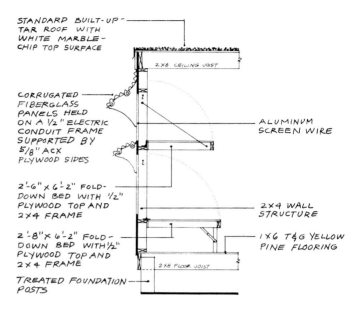

STANDARD BUILT-UP TAR ROOF WITH WHITE MARBLE-CHIP TOP SURFACE

2X8 CEILING JOIST

CORRUGATED FIBERGLASS PANELS HELD ON A ½" ELECTRIC CONDUIT FRAME SUPPORTED BY 5/8" ACX PLYWOOD SIDES

ALUMINUM SCREEN WIRE

2'-6" X 6'-2" FOLD-DOWN BED WITH ½" PLYWOOD TOP AND 2X4 FRAME

2X4 WALL STRUCTURE

2'-8" X 6'-2" FOLD-DOWN BED WITH ½" PLYWOOD TOP AND 2X4 FRAME

1X6 T&G YELLOW PINE FLOORING

2X8 FLOOR JOIST

TREATED FOUNDATION POSTS

Kitchen/dining module

The kitchen/dining module, shown below, provides 3' x 3' countertop facilities for cooking and washing. Once the meal is prepared, four flaps are unfolded to provide table space for dining for eight. The four lower bunk beds, folded down, can make seats for the table.

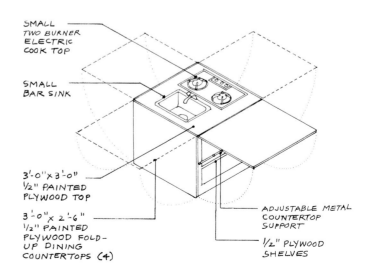

SMALL TWO BURNER ELECTRIC COOK TOP

SMALL BAR SINK

3'-0" X 3'-0" ½" PAINTED PLYWOOD TOP

3'-0" X 2'-6" ½" PAINTED PLYWOOD FOLD-UP DINING COUNTERTOPS (4)

ADJUSTABLE METAL COUNTERTOP SUPPORT

½" PLYWOOD SHELVES

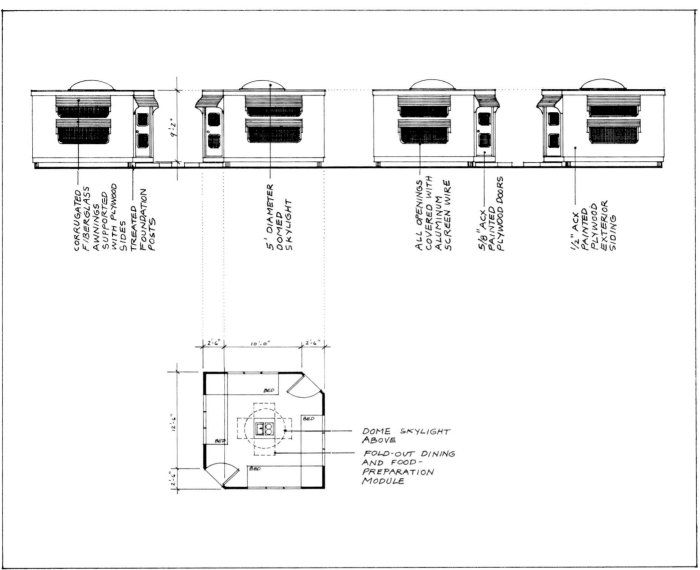

CORRUGATED FIBERGLASS AWNINGS SUPPORTED WITH PLYWOOD SIDES

TREATED FOUNDATION POSTS

5' DIAMETER DOMED SKYLIGHT

ALL OPENINGS COVERED WITH ALUMINUM SCREEN WIRE

5/8" ACX PAINTED PLYWOOD DOORS

1/2" ACX PAINTED PLYWOOD EXTERIOR SIDING

9'-2"

2'-6"   10'-0"   2'-6"

12'-6"

2'-6"

BED
BED
BED
BED

DOME SKYLIGHT ABOVE

FOLD-OUT DINING AND FOOD-PREPARATION MODULE

Plans and Elevations

Pattern

A smooth plywood exterior, the flat roof, the bubble skylight, and the hoods over the screened windows give a factory-made, modern, International Style look to the Picnic House. It resembles a little machine or appliance and, thus, might be painted any color and look interesting.

The pattern illustrates how easy it would be to construct this building: 2x4 stud walls, with painted plywood siding on a deck structured with 2x8 joists, with a roof of 2x8 rafters. The dome skylight should be available through a plastics distributor listed in the Yellow Pages.

Architect's Studio

11'-6" x 11'-6"
132 square feet

On a beautiful wooded ledge, just far enough away from his house to make it a separate place, and just close enough to make it a short walk, architect David Minch has carefully crafted himself a tiny studio in the Adirondack Mountains style. The building is included here because it is both a comfortable workplace and because it exhibits such excellent craftsmanship. Because it is so small and because no one task is too large, the builder(s) can use extreme patience and care in its construction. David Minch learned woodworking by constructing a 40-foot Valiant 40 sailing yacht, taking three years of fourteen-hour work days to do so. His studio, built later and in a style totally distinct from that of his boat, exhibits the same profuse love of the craft of building.

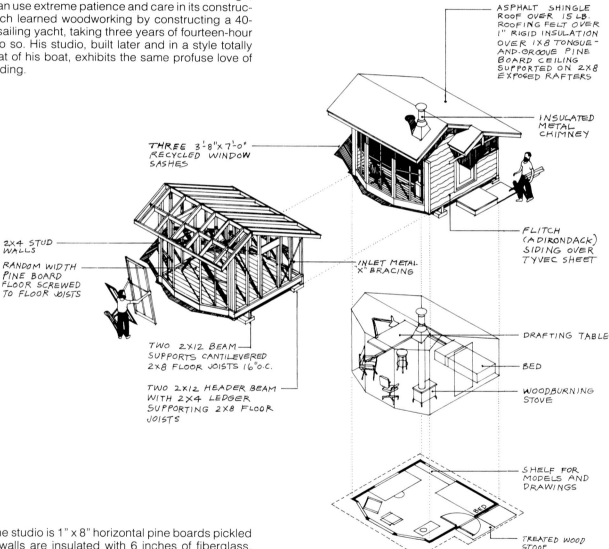

ASPHALT SHINGLE ROOF OVER 15 LB. ROOFING FELT OVER 1" RIGID INSULATION OVER 1X8 TONGUE-AND-GROOVE PINE BOARD CEILING SUPPORTED ON 2X8 EXPOSED RAFTERS

INSULATED METAL CHIMNEY

THREE 3'-8"X7'-0" RECYCLED WINDOW SASHES

2X4 STUD WALLS

RANDOM WIDTH PINE BOARD FLOOR SCREWED TO FLOOR JOISTS

INLET METAL "X" BRACING

FLITCH (ADIRONDACK) SIDING OVER TYVEC SHEET

TWO 2X12 BEAM SUPPORTS CANTILEVERED 2X8 FLOOR JOISTS 16"O.C.

TWO 2X12 HEADER BEAM WITH 2X4 LEDGER SUPPORTING 2X8 FLOOR JOISTS

DRAFTING TABLE

BED

WOODBURNING STOVE

SHELF FOR MODELS AND DRAWINGS

TREATED WOOD STOOP

The interior of the studio is 1" x 8" horizontal pine boards pickled flat white. The walls are insulated with 6 inches of fiberglass, and the roof has 1 inch of rigid polyurethane foam on top of the ceiling boards. The floor is wide pine boards sanded smooth and stained red.

One of the keys to the Adirondack Mountains style is the use of rough-cut boards with the bark left on one edge, as siding. This siding is known as Adirondack siding, or "flitch" siding (the untrimmed boards are known as "flitches").

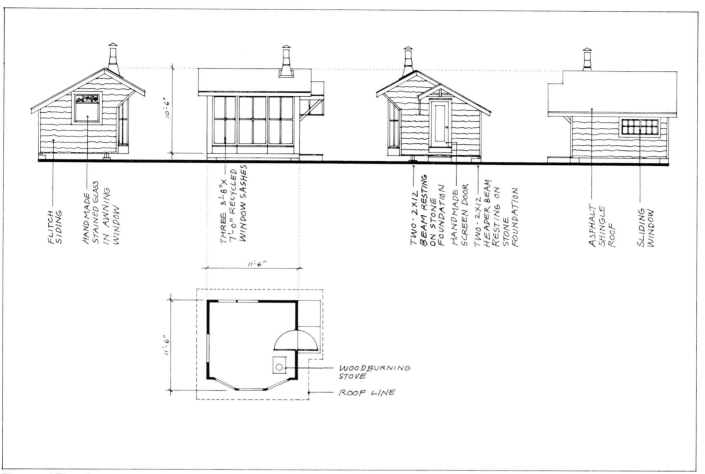

FLITCH SIDING

HANDMADE STAINED GLASS IN AWNING WINDOW

10'-6"

THREE 3'-8" X 7'-0" RECYCLED WINDOW SASHES

11'-6"

TWO - 2X12 BEAM RESTING ON STONE FOUNDATION

HANDMADE SCREEN DOOR

TWO - 2X12 HEADER BEAM RESTING ON STONE FOUNDATION

ASPHALT SHINGLE ROOF

SLIDING WINDOW

11'-6"

— WOODBURNING STOVE

— ROOF LINE

Plans and Elevations

Stained-glass window detail

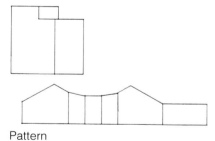

Pattern

The studio was designed around three large used fixed windows and two openable ones. David wanted the building to last for a very long time even though it might go untended, so he used flashing and caulking extensively and steeply sloped the windowsills.

The window detail shown in the photograph above illustrates the care given every detail of the construction. The flitch siding perfectly abuts the window trim, and the flashing line on the top trim piece is narrow and parallel. A stained-glass window was commissioned from artist Jean Whelan, a friend whose stained-glass work rivals David's woodworking ability.

Guest House

11' x 9'
99 square feet

This guest house was originally a tiny storage outbuilding, con-structed in the same style and with the same materials as its adjacent main house and converted in 1978 by New York sculptor Anthony Krauss. It is special because of its size, just large enough for a bed, a desk, and some cooking facilities. The painted tin roof with cupola, and the rose arbor give the building a wonderfully cozy domestic character.

A renovation from a storage building to a guest house was accomplished primarily with a broom, paint, some furniture, and simple built-in painted pine and plywood shelves. The house will sleep one or two guests quite comfortably and also provide facilities for Mr. Krauss to use a quiet backyard retreat for his work.

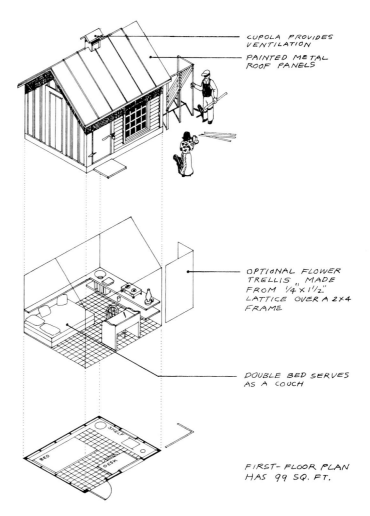

CUPOLA PROVIDES VENTILATION

PAINTED METAL ROOF PANELS

OPTIONAL FLOWER TRELLIS MADE FROM 1/4" x 1 1/2" LATTICE OVER A 2x4 FRAME

DOUBLE BED SERVES AS A COUCH

FIRST-FLOOR PLAN HAS 99 SQ. FT.

147

The guest house kitchen area is made with ¾" painted plywood shelves filled with catalog-ordered camper equipment, an electric hotplate, an oil lamp, and other pieces of kitchenware bought at hardware stores. A small area for washing and towel storage is included. The 1'-4" wide countertop and shelf unit can be made from one piece of 4' x 8' plywood screwed together and to the existing wall. A gas-operated camper stove can be used to replace the hot plate if electricity is not available.

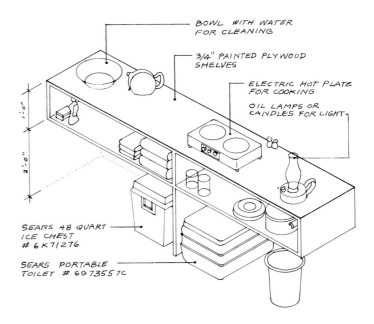

BOWL WITH WATER
FOR CLEANING

3/4" PAINTED PLYWOOD
SHELVES

ELECTRIC HOT PLATE
FOR COOKING

OIL LAMPS OR
CANDLES FOR LIGHT

SEARS 48 QUART
ICE CHEST
6K7/276

SEARS PORTABLE
TOILET # 6G73557C

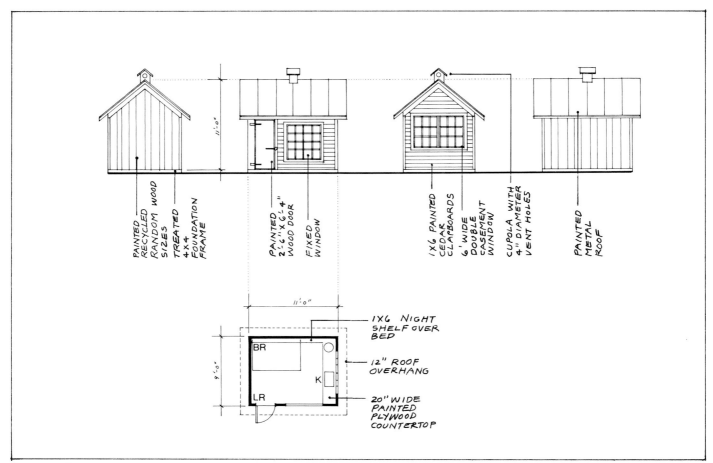

Plans and Elevations

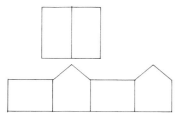

Pattern

The guest house is made from a hodgepodge of available siding materials, secondhand windows, and a handmade door, painted semigloss white. The roof is metal painted with a rust-proofing maroon-colored high-gloss paint. The interior is painted all white to match the exterior and to psychologically "increase" the sense of space.

Poetry House

6' x 4'-4"
26 square feet

Carol Anthony is a gifted Connecticut artist whose best work is often conceived after a lengthy period of quietness, reading or writing, in her humble Poetry House. "Solitude," she says, "is necessary nourishment for any creative process to begin."

Her Poetry House is an old weathered two-hole outhouse that she has beautifully, lovingly remodeled, with much help from her friend, furnituremaker Tommy Simpson, into a very pleasant little reading room. She calls it "a small, intimate slice of prose but representative of the bigger conversation of what I'm all about."

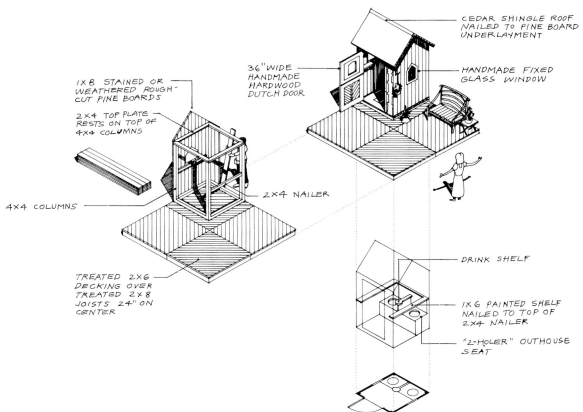

CEDAR SHINGLE ROOF NAILED TO PINE BOARD UNDERLAYMENT

36" WIDE HANDMADE HARDWOOD DUTCH DOOR

HANDMADE FIXED GLASS WINDOW

1 X 8 STAINED OR WEATHERED ROUGH-CUT PINE BOARDS

2 X 4 TOP PLATE RESTS ON TOP OF 4X4 COLUMNS

4 X 4 COLUMNS

2 X 4 NAILER

TREATED 2X6 DECKING OVER TREATED 2 X 8 JOISTS 24" ON CENTER

DRINK SHELF

1 X 6 PAINTED SHELF NAILED TO TOP OF 2 X 4 NAILER

"2-HOLER" OUTHOUSE SEAT

The history of Poetry House is a lesson in itself. This dilapidated, unused little outbuilding was given a new life—new use and an appropriate new rennovation with some elbow grease and poetic imagination.

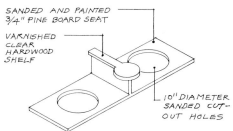

SANDED AND PAINTED
3/4" PINE BOARD SEAT

VARNISHED
CLEAR
HARDWOOD
SHELF

10" DIAMETER
SANDED CUT-
OUT HOLES

The interior of Poetry House has a fresh coat of gloss white paint, two fixed glass windows at seat level, framed artwork, fresh-cut flowers, and just enough carpeting and pillows to accommodate a comfortable one- or two-hour reading session. Its shelves can hold as many books as needed, and a drink can be stored on an armrest between the two seats, now pillowed.

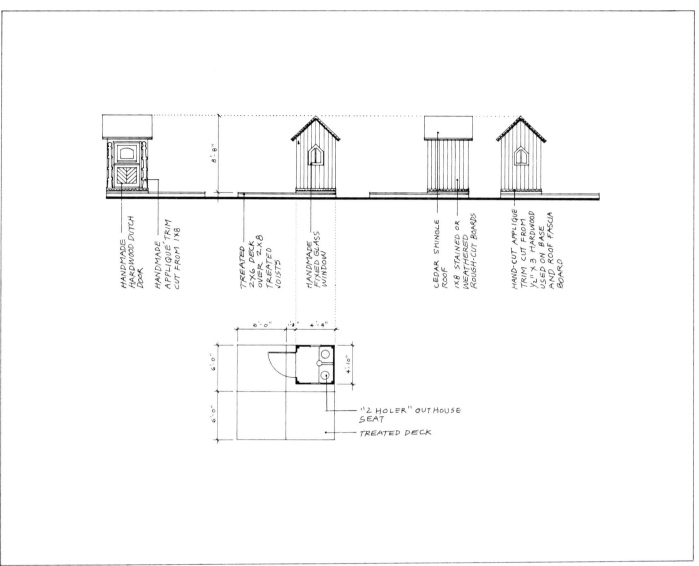

HANDMADE HARDWOOD DUTCH DOOR

HANDMADE APPLIQUE' TRIM CUT FROM 1X8

TREATED 2X6 DECK OVER 2X8 TREATED JOISTS

HANDMADE FIXED GLASS WINDOW

CEDAR SHINGLE ROOF

1X8 STAINED OR WEATHERED ROUGH-CUT BOARDS

HAND-CUT APPLIQUE TRIM CUT FROM ½"X 3 HARDWOOD USED ON BASE AND ROOF FASCIA BOARD

8'-8"

6'-0"   1'-8"   4'-4"

6'-0"

4'-10"

6'-0"

"2 HOLER" OUTHOUSE SEAT

TREATED DECK

Plans and Elevations

Pattern

The exterior of Poetry House is weathered rough-cut pine boards and cedar shingles, cleverly embellished with wood carvings by Tommy Simpson. It sits on a 10'x10' platform that gives the tiny building some stature and allows the interior, contemplative space to spill outside.

Tiny Roadside Houses

1950s Ranch House

12' x 9'
108 square feet

This classy little pink house with white trim sits just north of the Rappahannock River Bridge in a small development of tiny houses near Whitestone, Virginia. A 1960s Cadillac, completely dwarfing the house, is usually parked in the driveway.

Even though the house is tiny, it manages to exhibit most of the characteristics of a 1950s ranch house. On the exterior, first one sees the Cadillac, then the picture window, then the charcoal gray pyramidal roof and the pink clapboard siding, and on the interior, the drapes and the overstuffed furniture aimed at the TV. In fact, the lack of a dining table indicates that many TV dinners are probably consumed on the ever popular TV trays.

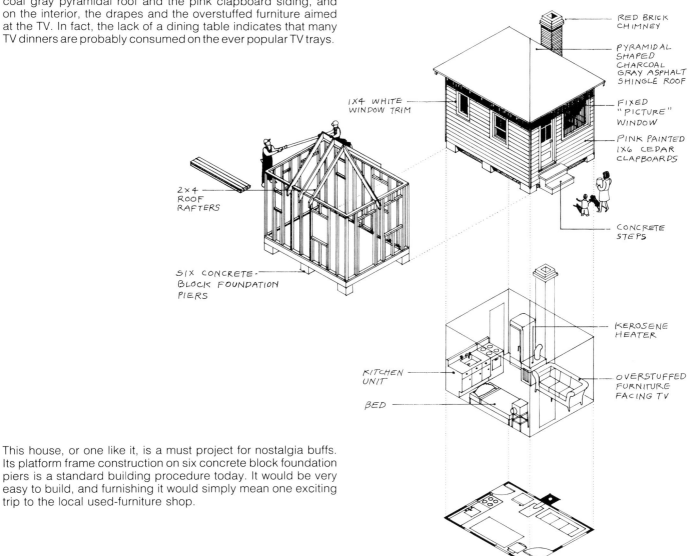

RED BRICK CHIMNEY

PYRAMIDAL SHAPED CHARCOAL GRAY ASPHALT SHINGLE ROOF

FIXED "PICTURE" WINDOW

PINK PAINTED 1X6 CEDAR CLAPBOARDS

1X4 WHITE WINDOW TRIM

2X4 ROOF RAFTERS

CONCRETE STEPS

SIX CONCRETE-BLOCK FOUNDATION PIERS

KEROSENE HEATER

OVERSTUFFED FURNITURE FACING TV

KITCHEN UNIT

BED

This house, or one like it, is a must project for nostalgia buffs. Its platform frame construction on six concrete block foundation piers is a standard building procedure today. It would be very easy to build, and furnishing it would simply mean one exciting trip to the local used-furniture shop.

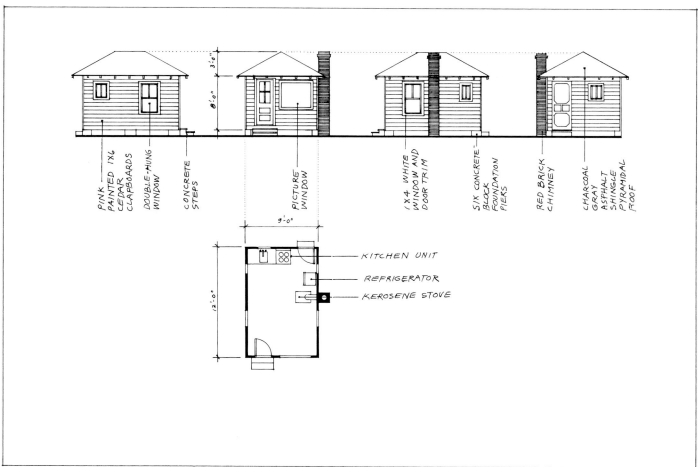

Plans and Elevations

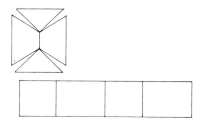

Pattern

The primary materials of the ranch house are pink painted clapboards, 1x4 white painted window and door trim, and a charcoal gray asphalt shingle roof over 2x4 rafters. All the windows and doors are standard types and sizes. This house requires, of course, a well, electricity, a kerosene stove, and an outhouse. The outhouse should be hidden because it is definitely not a 1950s item. The Cadillac is.

Catskill Motor Court built 1949

Motel Unit

15' x 12'
180 square feet

There are enough interesting tiny motel units in America to fill an endless number of books. The motel unit shown here is located in the Catskill Mountains of New York State and was chosen because it is a straightforward, prototypical example of a motel unit, the likes of which were built mostly in the 1940s and 1950s.

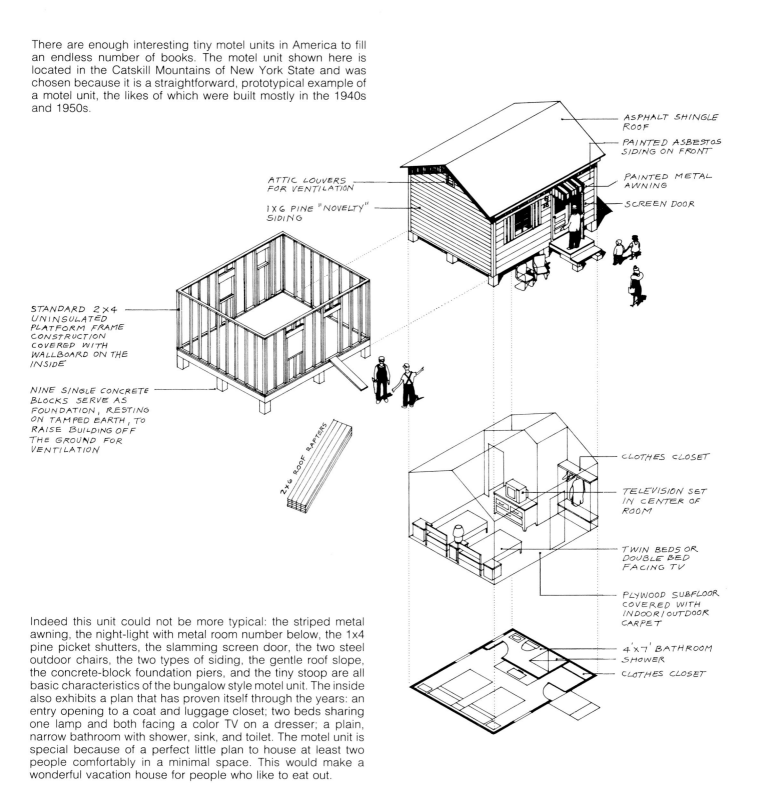

ATTIC LOUVERS FOR VENTILATION

1X6 PINE "NOVELTY" SIDING

STANDARD 2X4 UNINSULATED PLATFORM FRAME CONSTRUCTION COVERED WITH WALLBOARD ON THE INSIDE

NINE SINGLE CONCRETE BLOCKS SERVE AS FOUNDATION, RESTING ON TAMPED EARTH, TO RAISE BUILDING OFF THE GROUND FOR VENTILATION

2x6 ROOF RAFTERS

ASPHALT SHINGLE ROOF

PAINTED ASBESTOS SIDING ON FRONT

PAINTED METAL AWNING

SCREEN DOOR

CLOTHES CLOSET

TELEVISION SET IN CENTER OF ROOM

TWIN BEDS OR DOUBLE BED FACING TV

PLYWOOD SUBFLOOR COVERED WITH INDOOR/OUTDOOR CARPET

4'X7' BATHROOM
SHOWER
CLOTHES CLOSET

Indeed this unit could not be more typical: the striped metal awning, the night-light with metal room number below, the 1x4 pine picket shutters, the slamming screen door, the two steel outdoor chairs, the two types of siding, the gentle roof slope, the concrete-block foundation piers, and the tiny stoop are all basic characteristics of the bungalow style motel unit. The inside also exhibits a plan that has proven itself through the years: an entry opening to a coat and luggage closet; two beds sharing one lamp and both facing a color TV on a dresser; a plain, narrow bathroom with shower, sink, and toilet. The motel unit is special because of a perfect little plan to house at least two people comfortably in a minimal space. This would make a wonderful vacation house for people who like to eat out.

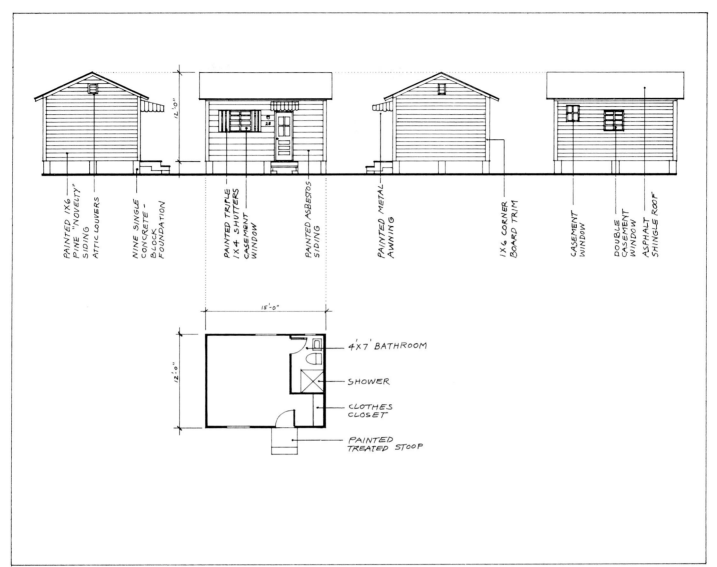

Plans and Elevations

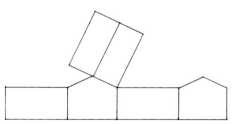

Pattern

The motel unit is sided with regular 1x6 painted pine novelty boards with the more impressive painted asbestos siding used on the front. Windows are small casements because the room is usually used only at night. The unit is raised off the ground on nine concrete-block piers to get proper air circulation for cooling and to prevent rotting of the floor structure. The motel unit is another project that would be fast and easy to build.

School-Bus Shelter

2'-4" x 2'-4"
5.5 square feet

This little building has to be the tiniest of all the tiny houses. It holds two children but only if they are standing. After much research this roadside structure has been identified as a shelter for two children waiting for their school bus in an upstate New York town.

The older child gets the high window and the younger gets the low—allowing both to see the school bus coming. The shelter is uninsulated and unheated (there is no room) but serves to cut the fierce north winds in winter and keep the children dry during rainstorms.

This shelter is a poignant example of American folk architecture, showing care for its inhabitants and expressing this in its form. It was built from painted scrap wood, an old piece of roll roofing for the building's cap, and junked car windows nailed to the exterior wall. The door handle is a simple wooden turn button.

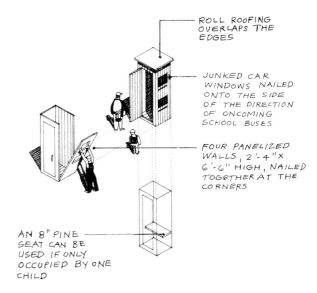

ROLL ROOFING OVERLAPS THE EDGES

JUNKED CAR WINDOWS NAILED ONTO THE SIDE OF THE DIRECTION OF ONCOMING SCHOOL BUSES

FOUR PANELIZED WALLS, 2'-4" X 6'-6" HIGH, NAILED TOGETHER AT THE CORNERS

AN 8" PINE SEAT CAN BE USED IF ONLY OCCUPIED BY ONE CHILD

Autonomous House

31' x 12'
324 square feet

One of the most technologically advanced dwelling units, short of the space capsules, is the Autonomous House shown here. It was developed and built in 1979 by Ted Bakewell III and Michael Jantzen (designer of the Picnic House, page 139) as a mobile home completely able to support itself, free from utility connections, with provisions for every domestic function. It was published in *Popular Science* magazine in April 1980.

The unit is heated passively by a small sunspace that doubles as an entry air lock. This system is backed up by an incinerator, which uses junk mail among its fuels, and a small woodburning stove. Insulation is primarily 3½ inches of urea-formaldehyde foam covered with a 1-inch interior layer of cellulose-based fireproofing/sound-absorbing material. Electrical power is dependent upon photovoltaics and battery storage.

Food preparation begins with a superinsulated refrigerator and ends with cooking over an alcohol burner (no electricity). Water is obtained from rain collected from gutters and delivered into a flexible vinyl "bladder." A 15-minute rain can capture over a month's supply of water. Once the water is used, it is piped to an under-floor gray-water storage tank where it is filtered for future limited reuse. Pressure to move the water through the pipes is generated with manually operated pumps.

The Autonomous House is unique in many ways but the most profound is its use of building components in new ways. For example, silo sections are used for the roof, space lamps as low-energy lighting, plastic swimming pool decking as flooring and wall covering, and ceiling mounted zippered canvas for storage space pouches. The design and fabrication of the Autonomous House exhibits the best of American do-it-yourself ingenuity combined with space-age high-tech thinking.

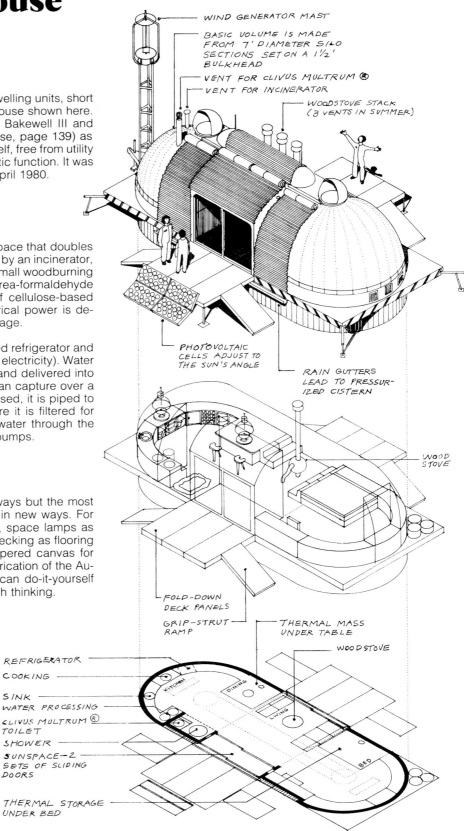

WIND GENERATOR MAST

BASIC VOLUME IS MADE FROM 7' DIAMETER SILO SECTIONS SET ON A 1½' BULKHEAD

VENT FOR CLIVUS MULTRUM ®

VENT FOR INCINERATOR

WOODSTOVE STACK (3 VENTS IN SUMMER)

PHOTOVOLTAIC CELLS ADJUST TO THE SUN'S ANGLE

RAIN GUTTERS LEAD TO PRESSUR- IZED CISTERN

WOOD STOVE

FOLD-DOWN DECK PANELS

GRIP-STRUT RAMP

THERMAL MASS UNDER TABLE

WOODSTOVE

REFRIGERATOR

COOKING

SINK

WATER PROCESSING

CLIVUS MULTRUM ® TOILET

SHOWER

SUNSPACE-2 SETS OF SLIDING DOORS

THERMAL STORAGE UNDER BED

KITCHEN

DINING

LIVING

BED

The diagram below shows how the Autonomous House passively heats itself during the winter months. Air is heated on the sun side of the building, is ducted into the building, it warms the space from the periphery, then moves to the sun side to be heated again.

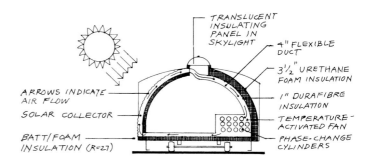

Wintertime heating diagram

Living room

Dining area

Kitchen

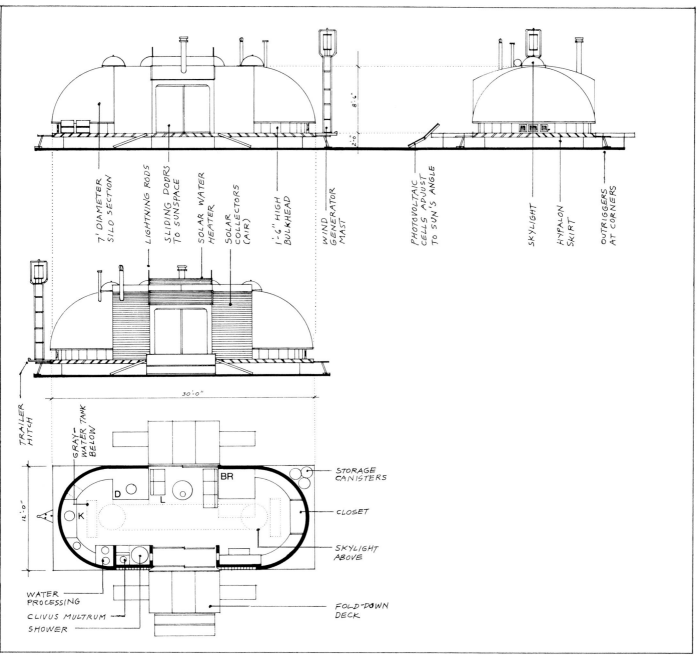

Labels in the drawing:

7' DIAMETER SILO SECTION
LIGHTNING RODS
SLIDING DOORS TO SUNSPACE
SOLAR WATER HEATER
SOLAR COLLECTORS (AIR)
1'-6" HIGH BULKHEAD
WIND GENERATOR MAST
PHOTOVOLTAIC CELLS ADJUST TO SUN'S ANGLE
SKYLIGHT
HYPALON SKIRT
OUTRIGGERS AT CORNERS

8'-6"
2'-0"

30'-0"
12'-0"

TRAILER HITCH
GRAY-WATER TANK BELOW
BR
D
L
K
STORAGE CANISTERS
CLOSET
SKYLIGHT ABOVE
WATER PROCESSING
CLIVUS MULTRUM
SHOWER
FOLD-DOWN DECK

Plans and Elevations

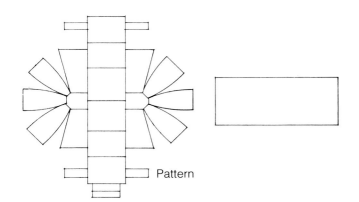

Pattern

The dimensions of the Autonomous House were dictated by the maximum highway requirements of 14 feet in width, 13 feet in height, and 10,000 pounds in weight. Lightweight silo components formed the one-quarter-sphere shell parts, mounted on a mobile-office chassis suitable for towing. All components were chosen for their light weight.

The designers stress that the unit is far from perfect. It is necessary to carry away much user refuse, to carry in fuel for the woodstove, and there is no provision for homegrown food. Both see their collaboration as a demonstration in what is possible now and where our research might take us in the future.

Fisherman's Shack

16' x 12'
192 square feet

Wherever there is water there are fishermen's shacks, and often they can be converted into living quarters. This is especially true along the seacoast in the state of Maine. Tiny lobster fishing shacks abound Down East and are often available to anyone with enough time and imagination to convert a tiny 16' x 12' shed into a home.

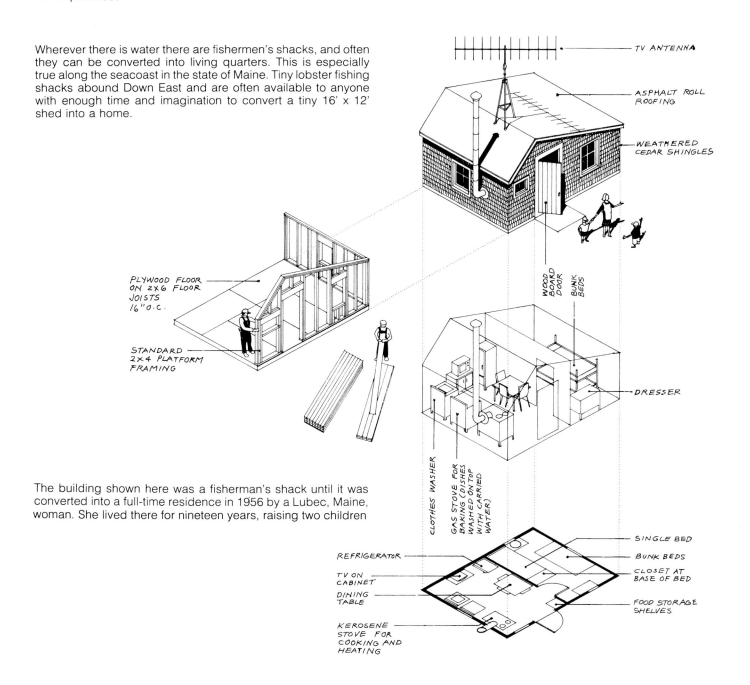

PLYWOOD FLOOR ON 2x6 FLOOR JOISTS 16" O.C.

STANDARD 2x4 PLATFORM FRAMING

TV ANTENNA

ASPHALT ROLL ROOFING

WEATHERED CEDAR SHINGLES

WOOD BOARD DOOR

BUNK BEDS

DRESSER

CLOTHES WASHER

GAS STOVE FOR BAKING (DISHES WASHED ON TOP WITH CARRIED WATER)

REFRIGERATOR

TV ON CABINET

DINING TABLE

KEROSENE STOVE FOR COOKING AND HEATING

SINGLE BED

BUNK BEDS

CLOSET AT BASE OF BED

FOOD STORAGE SHELVES

The building shown here was a fisherman's shack until it was converted into a full-time residence in 1956 by a Lubec, Maine, woman. She lived there for nineteen years, raising two children

and a host of pets. The tiny house had most modern conveniences except running water, which was hauled from a nearby spring. Television, washer/dryer, two types of cooking stoves, and living, dining, and sleeping areas for three all worked well. What was amazing was how all the furniture and appliances were arranged in the 192-square-foot space to accommodate movement and living patterns.

The drawing below illustrates the method used to side a fisherman's shack.

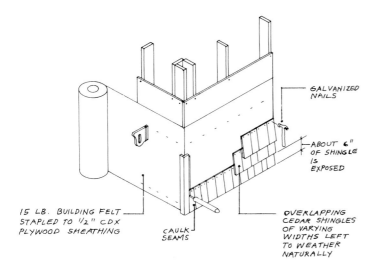

GALVANIZED NAILS

ABOUT 6" OF SHINGLE IS EXPOSED

15 LB. BUILDING FELT STAPLED TO 1/2" CDX PLYWOOD SHEATHING

CAULK SEAMS

OVERLAPPING CEDAR SHINGLES OF VARYING WIDTHS LEFT TO WEATHER NATURALLY

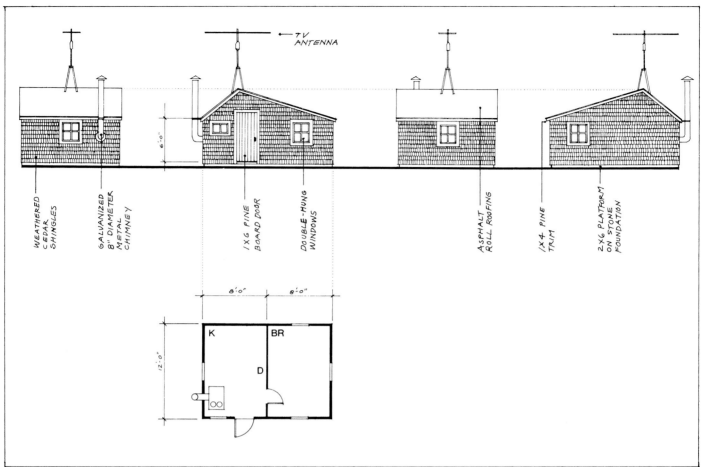

Plans and Elevations

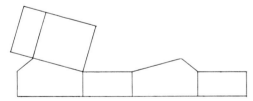

Pattern

Fishermen's shacks are part of the New England vernacular style. They are outbuildings of Cape Cods, saltboxes, and coastal farmhouses built in the straightforward English colonial style of the early settlers. There are no roof overhangs because the strong winds, common along the northeast coast, would endanger the roof. Tiny windows were common because they lost less heat, and funny shack shapes developed because the buildings were continually added on to over a period of time

The shack shown here was a 8' x 12' gable-roofed shed until it received an 8' x 12' saltbox addition sometime in the 1940s. Lace curtains and a TV antenna are inescapable signs of human habitation.

Tiny Houses as Art

Model by Allan Wexler

Dining Building with Window/Chairs

12' x 9'
108 square feet

The author of the works of art shown in this section is Allan Wexler, a New York City architect whose work combines small-scale architecture with his own original ideas concerning sculpture and industrial design. He is intrigued with the design of "little buildings for one human activity." He likes to find ways to make everyday rituals a celebration. His work includes columned, screened dining pavilions, gazebos, a wonderful tiny unit for summer showering, and outbuildings for picnicking and sleeping. Each is done with such humor and inventiveness that the viewer's imagination is stimulated. Referring to his work, he says, "I am inspired by the way a Japanese teahouse monumentalizes the drinking of tea."

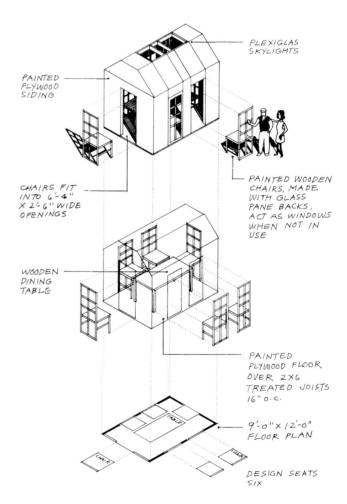

PLEXIGLAS SKYLIGHTS

PAINTED PLYWOOD SIDING

CHAIRS FIT INTO 6'-4" X 2'-6" WIDE OPENINGS

PAINTED WOODEN CHAIRS, MADE WITH GLASS PANE BACKS, ACT AS WINDOWS WHEN NOT IN USE

WOODEN DINING TABLE

PAINTED PLYWOOD FLOOR OVER 2X6 TREATED JOISTS 16" O.C.

9'-0" X 12'-0" FLOOR PLAN

DESIGN SEATS SIX

Dining Building with Window/Chairs has six entryways that frame six chairs after the guests are seated. The glass-paned chair backs become the windows of the building.

The idea that part of the structure (in this case the chair) can have double and often triple functions is important in designing tiny houses. Every inch of space must be used, and if a piece of the building can have many uses, the building itself is more effective. Dining Building with Window/Chairs is included here as a perfect realization of this idea. It has not yet been built; it might be impractical, but it is certainly inspiring and unique.

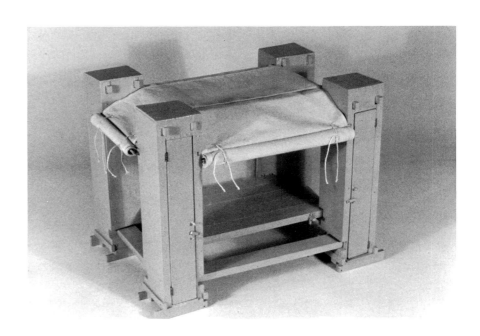

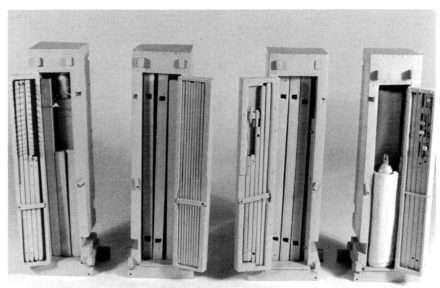

Model by Allan Wexler

Building for Picnicking

9' x 7'

63 square feet

When not in use, this building consists of four sea-blue columns standing apart on a lawn. In the spring, when opened and unpacked, the columns provide the materials for a lovely tiny house for picnics. Benches, table, and canopy are removed from the columns and erected between the column structure. The table can also double as a bed frame, turning the picnic house into a bedroom for summer sleeping (mosquito netting replaces the canvas canopy).

This is another more technological idea that lends itself to the building of tiny structures. One can imagine how the parts for a tiny house might be stored in similar locked columns on a vulnerable wilderness site.

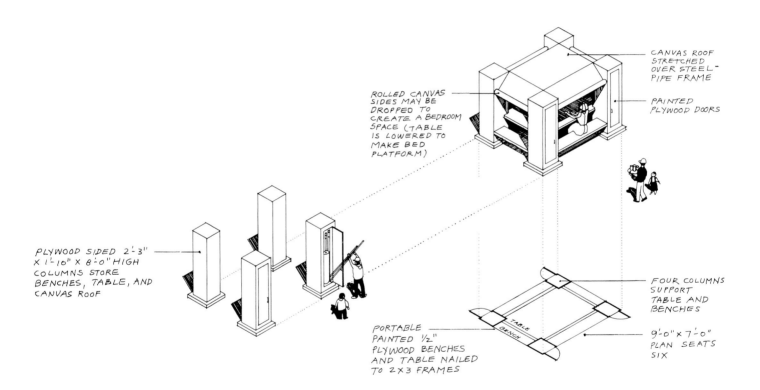

CANVAS ROOF STRETCHED OVER STEEL-PIPE FRAME

ROLLED CANVAS SIDES MAY BE DROPPED TO CREATE A BEDROOM SPACE (TABLE IS LOWERED TO MAKE BED PLATFORM)

PAINTED PLYWOOD DOORS

PLYWOOD SIDED 2'-3" X 1'-10" X 8'-0" HIGH COLUMNS STORE BENCHES, TABLE, AND CANVAS ROOF

FOUR COLUMNS SUPPORT TABLE AND BENCHES

PORTABLE PAINTED ½" PLYWOOD BENCHES AND TABLE NAILED TO 2X3 FRAMES

TABLE

BENCH

9'-0" X 7'-0" PLAN SEATS SIX

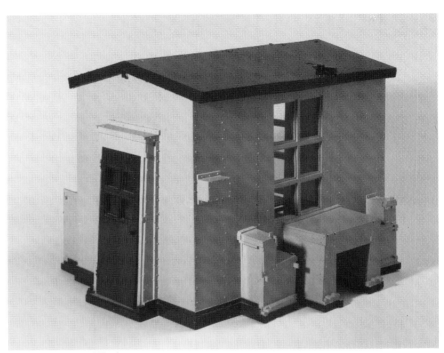

Model by Allan Wexler

Little Building for Two Activities

15' x 10' with storage extensions
150 square feet

This small building is a guest house that includes both a dining room and a bedroom. It is appealing because it acts on the modernist assumption that the functioning of the interior of a structure should be expressed on the exterior. Well, here it is: the unhidden furniture-storage volumes attached to the outside walls give a true indication of interior use—sleeping and dining.

This building is the most humorous of the three Wexler pieces, but it is also the most practical. One single, tiny, inexpensive space used for two living functions with storable furniture becomes a constantly changing stage set of ingenuity.

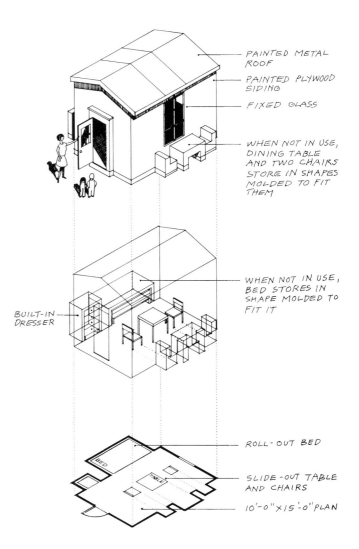

PAINTED METAL ROOF

PAINTED PLYWOOD SIDING

FIXED GLASS

WHEN NOT IN USE, DINING TABLE AND TWO CHAIRS STORE IN SHAPES MOLDED TO FIT THEM

WHEN NOT IN USE, BED STORES IN SHAPE MOLDED TO FIT IT

BUILT-IN DRESSER

ROLL-OUT BED

SLIDE-OUT TABLE AND CHAIRS

10'-0" x 15'-0" PLAN

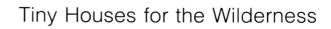

Tiny Houses for the Wilderness

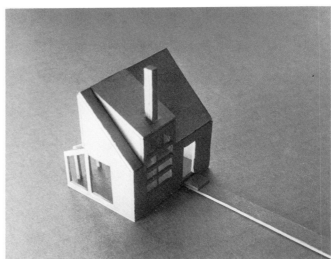

Model by Lester Walker

Cottage in the Woods

16' x 8' plus dining extension & sleeping loft
258 square feet

This little vacation house was designed by myself in 1978 for *Popular Mechanics* magazine. A four-week do-it-yourself project for about $2000 worth of materials. The plan includes two sleeping areas (one double and one single), the traditional living/dining/kitchen area, and a bathroom. All the fixtures are purchased from camping catalogs, and the heat, if necessary, is from a woodburning stove.

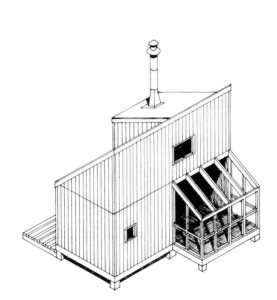

The house is styled to fit into the woods. The shape is borrowed from American vernacular buildings—the steep shed roof from barns and the dormer from early houses. The materials are chosen to enhance the style and setting. The Cottage in the Woods makes a great ski house (with insulation) or a perfect lakeside retreat.

All of the materials to build the house are bought, off the shelf, from low-budget lumberyards or house centers. Building methods are standard platform frame construction with 2x4 stud walls and 2x6 floor and roof joists.

The construction of this cottage would be an interesting project for a beginning housebuilder, with some carpentry experience, to undertake. The technology is simple and neat with just the right amount of complexity to keep the work interesting and educational.

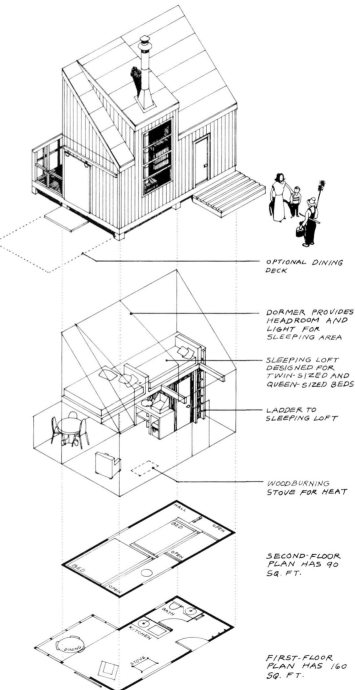

OPTIONAL DINING DECK

DORMER PROVIDES HEADROOM AND LIGHT FOR SLEEPING AREA

SLEEPING LOFT DESIGNED FOR TWIN-SIZED AND QUEEN-SIZED BEDS

LADDER TO SLEEPING LOFT

WOODBURNING STOVE FOR HEAT

SECOND-FLOOR PLAN HAS 90 SQ. FT.

FIRST-FLOOR PLAN HAS 160 SQ. FT.

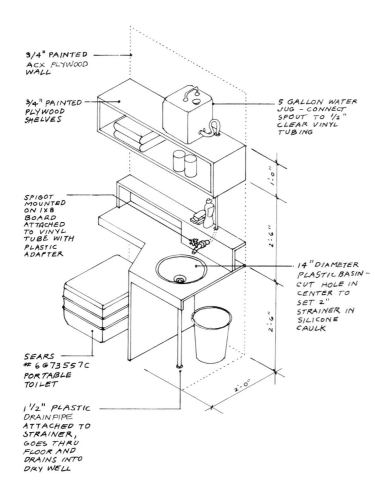

The bathrooms and kitchen in the cottage are unique in that they can be constructed with catalog camper equipment and a sheet of ¾" plywood. Each room can be fabricated by a novice homebuilder with no plumbing or electrical knowledge.

3/4" PAINTED ACX PLYWOOD WALL

3/4" PAINTED PLYWOOD SHELVES

5 GALLON WATER JUG - CONNECT SPOUT TO 1/2" CLEAR VINYL TUBING

SPIGOT MOUNTED ON 1X8 BOARD ATTACHED TO VINYL TUBE WITH PLASTIC ADAPTER

14" DIAMETER PLASTIC BASIN - CUT HOLE IN CENTER TO SET 2" STRAINER IN SILICONE CAULK

SEARS # 6G73557C PORTABLE TOILET

1½" PLASTIC DRAIN PIPE ATTACHED TO STRAINER, GOES THRU FLOOR AND DRAINS INTO DRY WELL

Bathroom

The kitchen and bathroom shown here can, of course, be adapted to fit other houses. They are an inexpensive alternative to a regular kitchen and bathroom that could cost tens of thousands of dollars (including the cost of a well). However, they do require a nearby source of water, such as a friend or a spring, and energy for hauling this water to the site.

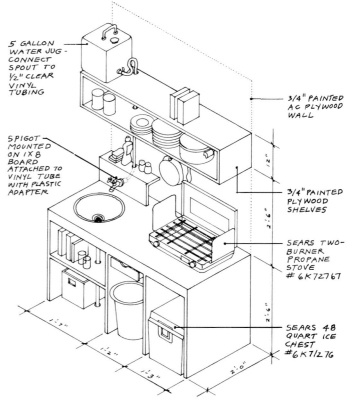

5 GALLON WATER JUG - CONNECT SPOUT TO 1/2" CLEAR VINYL TUBING

SPIGOT MOUNTED ON 1X8 BOARD ATTACHED TO VINYL TUBE WITH PLASTIC ADAPTER

3/4" PAINTED AC PLYWOOD WALL

3/4" PAINTED PLYWOOD SHELVES

SEARS TWO-BURNER PROPANE STOVE # 6K72767

SEARS 48 QUART ICE CHEST #6K7/276

Kitchen

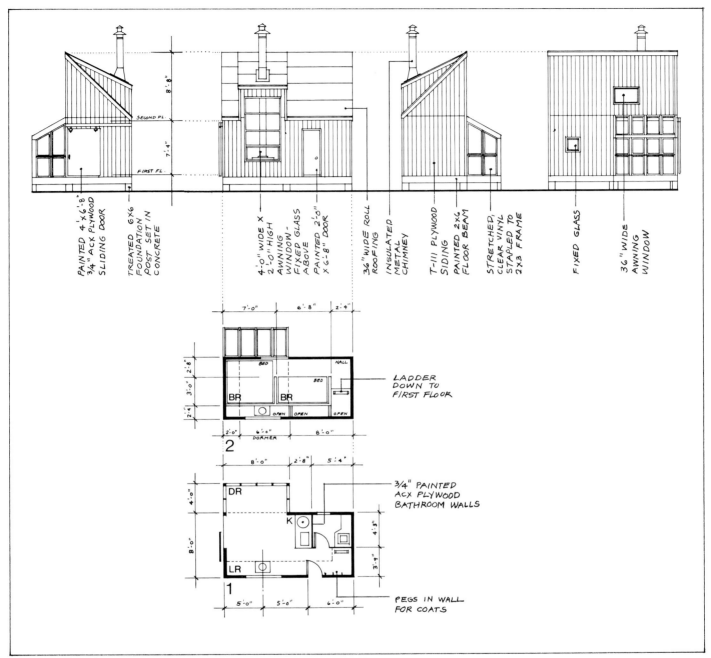

PAINTED 4'x6'-8"
3/4" ACX PLYWOOD
SLIDING DOOR

TREATED 6X6
FOUNDATION
POST SET IN
CONCRETE

4'-0"WIDE X
2'-0"HIGH
AWNING
WINDOW -
FIXED GLASS
ABOVE

PAINTED 2'-0"
X 6'-8" DOOR

36"WIDE ROLL
ROOFING

INSULATED
METAL
CHIMNEY

T-III PLYWOOD
SIDING

PAINTED 2x6
FLOOR BEAM

STRETCHED,
CLEAR VINYL
STAPLED TO
2X3 FRAME

FIXED GLASS

36"WIDE
AWNING
WINDOW

LADDER
DOWN TO
FIRST FLOOR

3/4" PAINTED
ACX PLYWOOD
BATHROOM WALLS

PEGS IN WALL
FOR COATS

Plans and Elevations

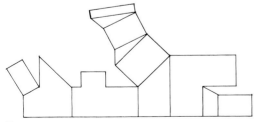

Pattern

Handmade House

20' x 12' plus two sleeping lofts
240 square feet

This tiny handmade cottage was built by fifty-three-year-old schoolteacher Mary Carrabba on a remote site near her home in Spokane, Washington. She calls it her mountain cabin.

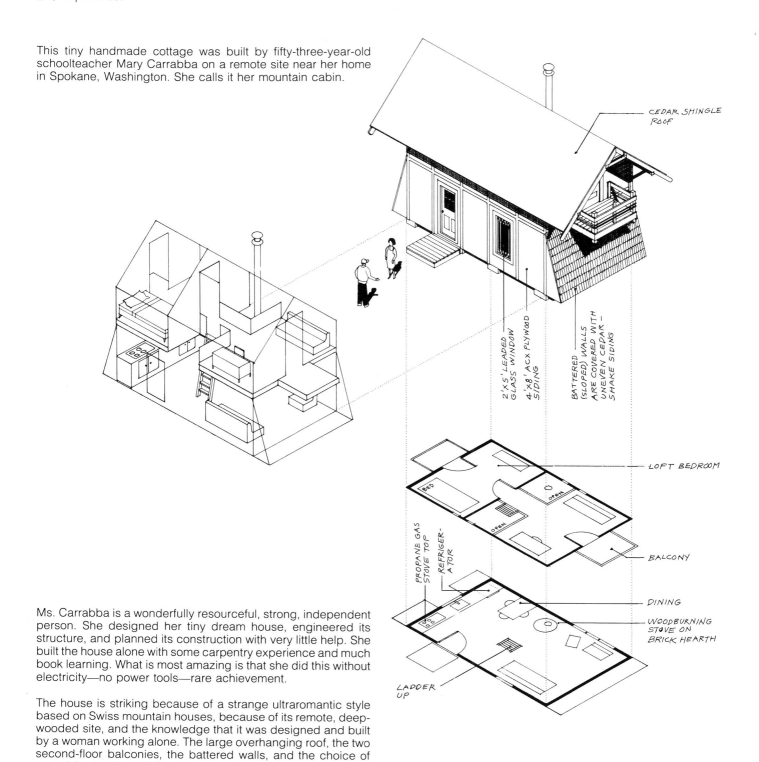

CEDAR SHINGLE ROOF

2'X5' LEADED GLASS WINDOW

4'X8' ACX PLYWOOD SIDING

BATTERED (SLOPED) WALLS ARE COVERED WITH UNEVEN CEDAR – SHAKE SIDING

LOFT BEDROOM

BALCONY

PROPANE GAS STOVE TOP

REFRIGER-ATOR

DINING

WOODBURNING STOVE ON BRICK HEARTH

LADDER UP

Ms. Carrabba is a wonderfully resourceful, strong, independent person. She designed her tiny dream house, engineered its structure, and planned its construction with very little help. She built the house alone with some carpentry experience and much book learning. What is most amazing is that she did this without electricity—no power tools—rare achievement.

The house is striking because of a strange ultraromantic style based on Swiss mountain houses, because of its remote, deep-wooded site, and the knowledge that it was designed and built by a woman working alone. The large overhanging roof, the two second-floor balconies, the battered walls, and the choice of materials give the building a rustic, woodsy character that would be hard to match.

The structure used by Mary Carrabba for her cottage is shown below. Note the eccentric positioning of the cantilevered 4x6 beams used to support the second-floor balconies.

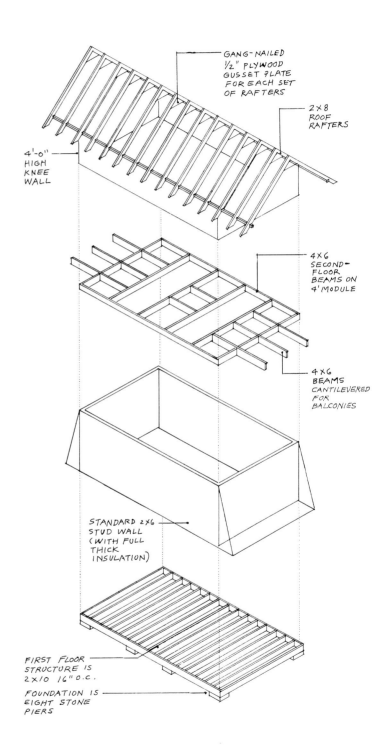

GANG-NAILED ½" PLYWOOD GUSSET PLATE FOR EACH SET OF RAFTERS

2×8 ROOF RAFTERS

4'-0" HIGH KNEE WALL

4×6 SECOND-FLOOR BEAMS ON 4' MODULE

4×6 BEAMS CANTILEVERED FOR BALCONIES

STANDARD 2×6 STUD WALL (WITH FULL THICK INSULATION)

FIRST FLOOR STRUCTURE IS 2×10 16" O.C.

FOUNDATION IS EIGHT STONE PIERS

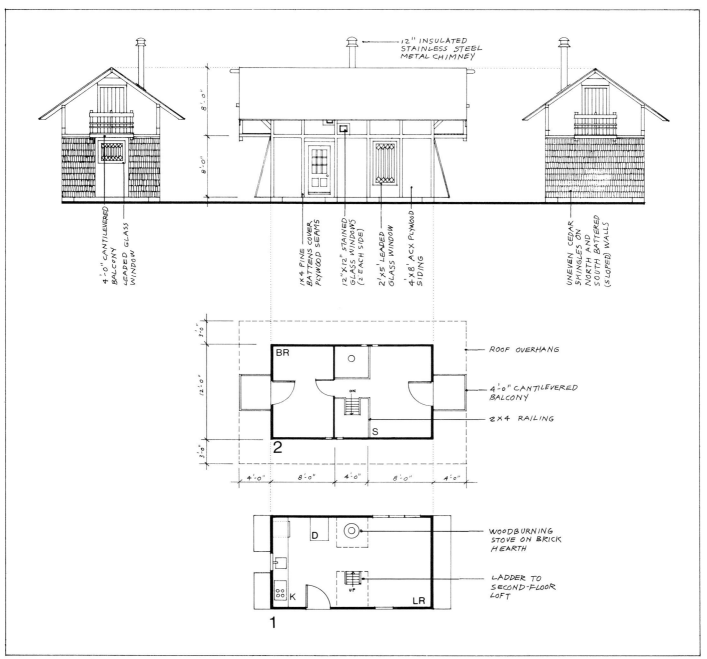

12" INSULATED STAINLESS STEEL METAL CHIMNEY

4'-0" CANTILEVERED BALCONY

LEADED GLASS WINDOW

1X4 PINE BATTENS COVER PLYWOOD SEAMS

12"X12" STAINED GLASS WINDOWS (2 EACH SIDE)

2'X5' LEADED GLASS WINDOW

4'X8' ACX PLYWOOD SIDING

UNEVEN CEDAR SHINGLES ON NORTH AND SOUTH BATTERED (SLOPED) WALLS

BR

ROOF OVERHANG

4'-0" CANTILEVERED BALCONY

2X4 RAILING

DN

S

2

WOODBURNING STOVE ON BRICK HEARTH

D

LADDER TO SECOND-FLOOR LOFT

UP

K

LR

1

Plans and Elevations

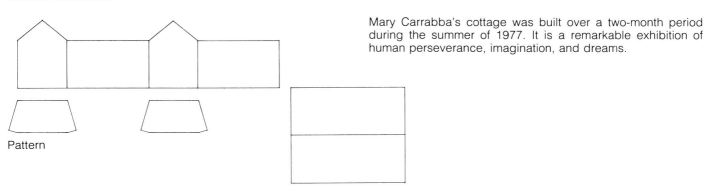

Pattern

Mary Carrabba's cottage was built over a two-month period during the summer of 1977. It is a remarkable exhibition of human perseverance, imagination, and dreams.

Recycled House

16' x 8' two stories
256 square feet

This tiny building was constructed by Graham Blackburn, a New York writer and fine furniture maker, with materials he removed from a nearby barn that was to be demolished. Blackburn was given the barn provided he remove it from its location. He decided to build a house reusing most of the barn's materials while adding some local fieldstone for a foundation, a new asphalt shingle roof, and new cedar clapboard siding.

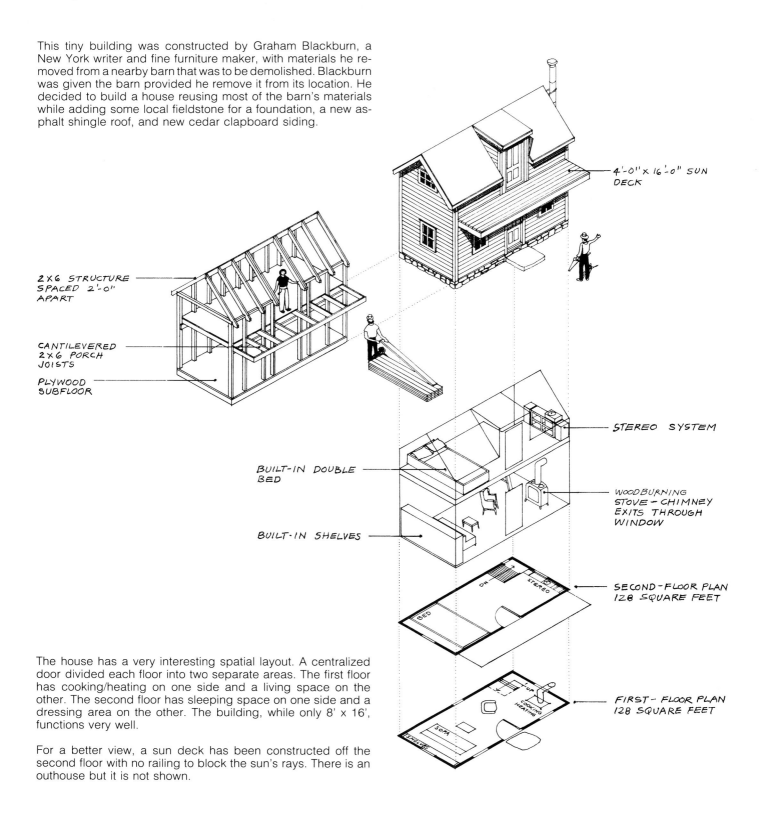

4'-0" x 16'-0" SUN DECK

2 X 6 STRUCTURE SPACED 2'-0" APART

CANTILEVERED 2 X 6 PORCH JOISTS

PLYWOOD SUBFLOOR

STEREO SYSTEM

BUILT-IN DOUBLE BED

WOODBURNING STOVE — CHIMNEY EXITS THROUGH WINDOW

BUILT-IN SHELVES

SECOND-FLOOR PLAN 128 SQUARE FEET

FIRST-FLOOR PLAN 128 SQUARE FEET

The house has a very interesting spatial layout. A centralized door divided each floor into two separate areas. The first floor has cooking/heating on one side and a living space on the other. The second floor has sleeping space on one side and a dressing area on the other. The building, while only 8' x 16', functions very well.

For a better view, a sun deck has been constructed off the second floor with no railing to block the sun's rays. There is an outhouse but it is not shown.

Sheathed and papered

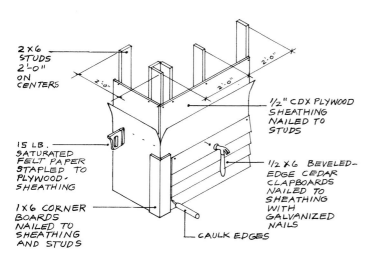

2 X 6
STUDS
2'-0"
ON
CENTERS

1/2" CDX PLYWOOD
SHEATHING
NAILED TO
STUDS

15 LB.
SATURATED
FELT PAPER
STAPLED TO
PLYWOOD·
SHEATHING

1/2 X 6 BEVELED-
EDGE CEDAR
CLAPBOARDS
NAILED TO
SHEATHING
WITH
GALVANIZED
NAILS

1 X 6 CORNER
BOARDS
NAILED TO
SHEATHING
AND STUDS

CAULK EDGES

After the frame was constructed with the reused barn materials it was sheathed and papered before being sided with new, store-bought, traditional materials. Standard construction methods were used, as the drawing to the left illustrates. The finished sided house was painted with two coats of a clear protective stain.

Taking apart an old building and constructing a new one with materials from the old is an economical but time-consuming project. Special skills and equipment are necessary in dismantling and transporting the old materials to a new site.

Siding completed

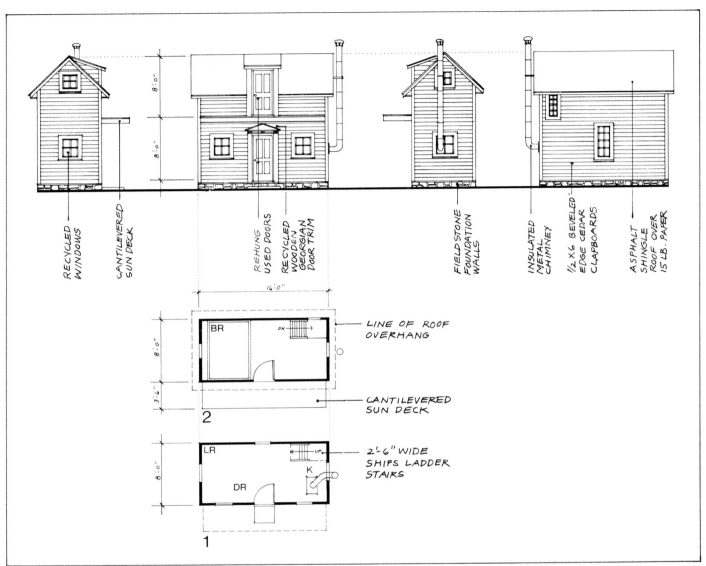

RECYCLED WINDOWS

CANTILEVERED SUN DECK

REHUNG USED DOORS

RECYCLED WOODEN GEORGIAN DOOR TRIM

FIELDSTONE FOUNDATION WALLS

INSULATED METAL CHIMNEY

½ X 6 BEVELED EDGE CEDAR CLAPBOARDS

ASPHALT SHINGLE ROOF OVER 15 LB. PAPER

16'0"

8'0"

3'6"

BR

DN

LINE OF ROOF OVERHANG

CANTILEVERED SUN DECK

2

8'0"

LR

UP

K

2'-6" WIDE SHIPS LADDER STAIRS

DR

1

Plans and Elevations

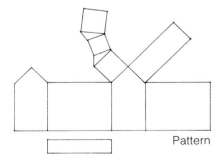

Pattern

With the exception of the cedar siding, the most expensive materials in this new tiny house were recycled from the old barn—structural members, floors, windows, doors, and interior wood cladding. If one is lucky enough to find an old unwanted building, it must be carefully studied to make sure it contains enough usable material to make dismantling and recycling worthwhile.

Shower side

Inside-Out House

9' x 6' plus outside kitchen and bath
54 square feet

One of the most clever houses in this book is this tiny windowless building, just as big as a double bed, built in 1967 by a young couple in Sharon, Connecticut, for shelter while they built the log cabin of their dreams nearby. It's called the Inside-Out House because all the living functions, except sleeping, occur on the outside periphery of the building.

A large overhanging roof protects L-shaped kitchen cabinets on two exterior walls and a shower on a third wall. A big door, usually open for ventilation, occupies the fourth wall. An enormous dining room, as large as all outdoors, is located adjacent to the big door. The living room, equally as large, is located adjacent to the kitchen. These rooms are defined primarily by trees but also by "negative windows" such as wicker trays, picture frames, and pieces of cloth hung from the trees. As David Bain, the owner/builder, expresses it, "Since we could see through our walls, we didn't need to see through our windows."

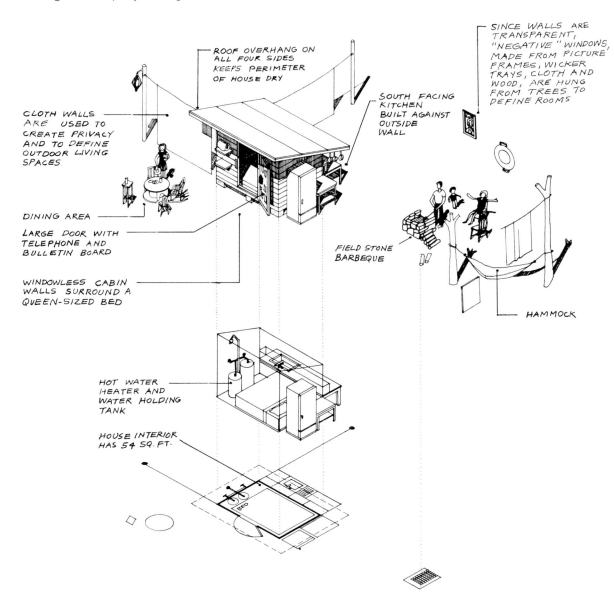

ROOF OVERHANG ON ALL FOUR SIDES KEEPS PERIMETER OF HOUSE DRY

SINCE WALLS ARE TRANSPARENT, "NEGATIVE" WINDOWS, MADE FROM PICTURE FRAMES, WICKER TRAYS, CLOTH AND WOOD, ARE HUNG FROM TREES TO DEFINE ROOMS

SOUTH FACING KITCHEN BUILT AGAINST OUTSIDE WALL

CLOTH WALLS ARE USED TO CREATE PRIVACY AND TO DEFINE OUTDOOR LIVING SPACES

DINING AREA

LARGE DOOR WITH TELEPHONE AND BULLETIN BOARD

FIELD STONE BARBEQUE

WINDOWLESS CABIN WALLS SURROUND A QUEEN-SIZED BED

HAMMOCK

HOT WATER HEATER AND WATER HOLDING TANK

HOUSE INTERIOR HAS 54 SQ. FT.

The kitchen of the Inside-Out House is arranged around the outside corner of the building—food storage with the refrigerator on one side and food preparation with the sink around the corner. Because the house has electricity and running water, the kitchen, though outside, is relatively modern. The work surfaces are made with pieces of inexpensive construction-grade lumber or scrap wood and is protected above with the wide roof overhang mentioned earlier.

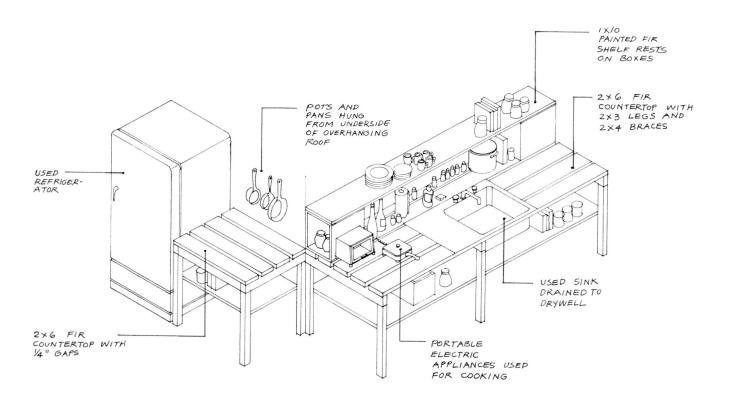

1×10
PAINTED FIR
SHELF RESTS
ON BOXES

2×6 FIR
COUNTERTOP WITH
2×3 LEGS AND
2×4 BRACES

POTS AND
PANS HUNG
FROM UNDERSIDE
OF OVERHANGING
ROOF

USED
REFRIGER-
ATOR

USED SINK
DRAINED TO
DRYWELL

2×6 FIR
COUNTERTOP WITH
¼" GAPS

PORTABLE
ELECTRIC
APPLIANCES USED
FOR COOKING

The Inside-Out House was meant to be temporary, inexpensive, and functional, so it was built with secondhand materials, such as the 4x4 and 4x6 telephone-pole cross pieces used for the frame (obtained from the local dump) and low-budget siding and roofing. It is truly an innovative tiny house, born of necessity.

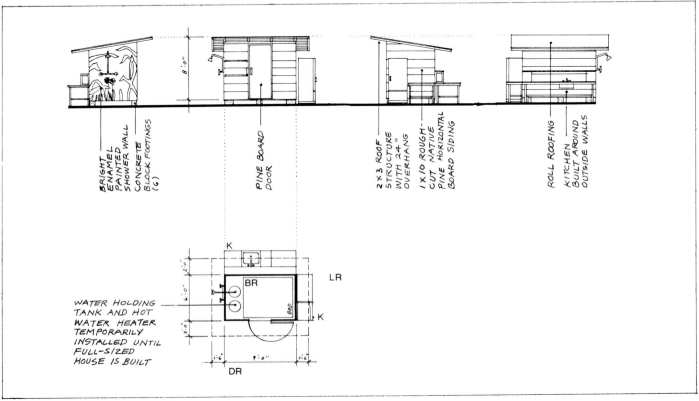

Plans and Elevations

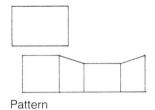

Pattern

Dune Shack

11' x 8'-6"
94 square feet

At the end of the nineteenth century, the United States Coast Guard patrolled the dangerous waters off Cape Cod near Provincetown by walking the beaches. In order to make their tour of duty more comfortable, they built tiny driftwood outbuildings in the dunes as quiet getaways from their base. They also built a few to hold cows and hens and other domestic animals.

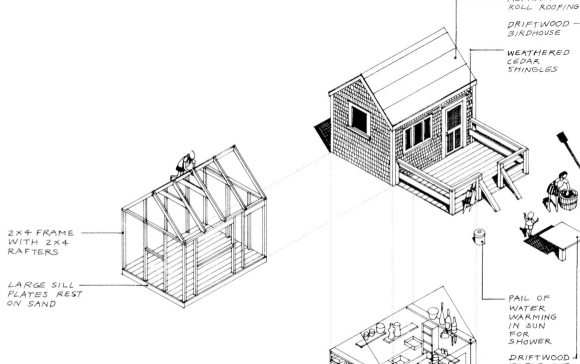

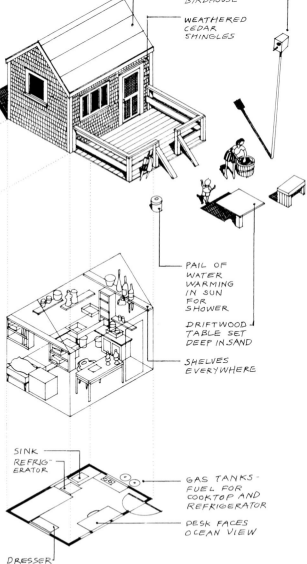

2×4 FRAME WITH 2×4 RAFTERS

LARGE SILL PLATES REST ON SAND

ASPHALT ROLL ROOFING

DRIFTWOOD BIRDHOUSE

WEATHERED CEDAR SHINGLES

PAIL OF WATER WARMING IN SUN FOR SHOWER

DRIFTWOOD TABLE SET DEEP IN SAND

SHELVES EVERYWHERE

SINK

REFRIGERATOR

GAS TANKS - FUEL FOR COOKTOP AND REFRIGERATOR

DESK FACES OCEAN VIEW

DRESSER

In the beginning of the 1900s some townspeople, anxious to spend more time on the desolate beaches and dunes, spent their summers constructing dune shacks of their own. By the 1920s a community of twenty to twenty-five tiny buildings existed along the dunes, back from the beaches, about an hour's walk from Provincetown. The shacks were inhabited then by naturalists, writers such as Eugene O'Neill, poets such as Harry Kemp, and artists. By the mid-1930's, the Coast Guard had left this part of the cape, and the Coast Guard station had slid into the sea. The shacks remained, lived in and maintained by the same inhabitants.

Today, about fifteen of these lovely weathered dune shacks still exist. The Cape Cod National Seashore of the United States Department of Interior is anxious to have them removed, but they are being challenged by the Peaked Hill Trust, a group of citizens who want to save the shacks.

The shack shown on these pages is owned by Hazel Hawthorne Werner, a naturalist in her eighties. She rents this shack and her other one, shown on pages 200 and 204, named Thalasa (Greek word meaning "sea"), to friends—people who appreciate the dunes and the simple style of living.

This dune shack is about 8 feet wide by 10 feet deep. A small potbelly stove is used for heating and cooking. It is a very special place, snuggled in between two small grassy dunes, facing the ocean. Everything, from the two sets of "French" doors (outside and screen) to the built-in bed in the back, is designed to take maximum advantage of the ocean view and prevailing summer breezes.

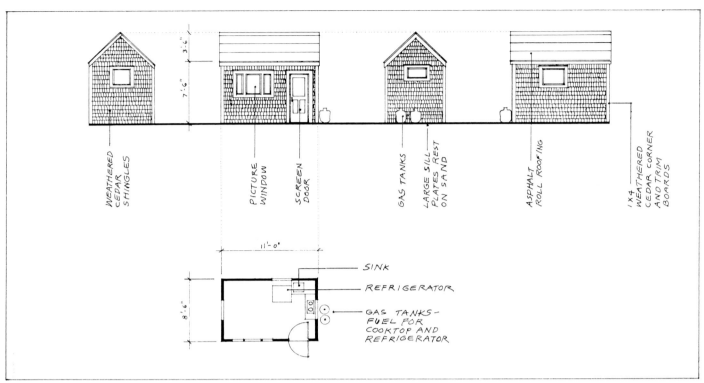

Plans and Elevations

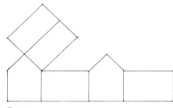

Pattern

The dune shacks were built on large wooden sill plates, resting on stones or sand. They were often dragged along the sand to a better site as the dunes shifted, much like the original Cape Cod houses.

Other primary materials included driftwood brought by the sea or more traditional wood siding and roofing brought by horse and cart or four-wheel-drive vehicle. Several wells were drilled in the 1930s, and each shack has an outhouse. Thalasa, above, used gas to fuel a small refrigerator and cooktop.

The Tiniest House

A story by Charles (Chic) Sale as told in 1929

The Specialist

Mr. President and Gentlemen:

You've heerd a lot of pratin' and prattlin' about this bein' the age of specialization. I'm a carpenter by trade. At one time I could of built a house, barn, church, or chicken coop. But I seen the need of a specialist in my line, so I studied her. I got her; she's mine. Gentlemen, you are face to face with the champion privy builder of Sangamon County.

Luke Harkins was my first customer. He heerd about me specializin' and decided to take a chance. I built fer him just the average eight family, three holer. With that job my reputation was made, and since then I have devoted all my time and thought to that special line. Of course, when business is slack, I do do a little paperhangin' on the side. But my heart is just in privy buildin'. And when I finish a job, I ain't through. I give all my customers six months' privy service free gratis. I explained this to Luke, and one day he calls me up and sez: "Lem, I wish you'd come out here; I'm havin' privy trouble."

So I gits in the car and drives out to Luke's place, and hid behind them Baldwins, where I could get a good view of the situation.

It was right in the middle of hayin' time, and them hired hands was goin' in there and stayin' anywheres from forty minutes to an hour. Think of that!

I sez: "Luke, you sure have got privy trouble." So I takes out my kit of tools and goes in to examine the structure.

First I looks at the catalogue hangin' there, thinkin' it might be that; but it wasn't even from a reckonized house. Then I looks at the seats proper, and I see what the trouble was. I had made them holes too durn comfortable. So I gets out a scroll saw and cuts 'em square with hard edges. Then I go back and takes up my position as before—me here, the Baldwins here, and the privy there. And I watched them hired hands goin' in and out for nearly two hours; and not one of them was stayin' more than four minutes.

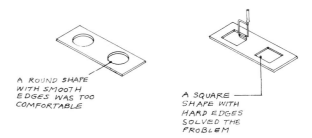

A ROUND SHAPE WITH SMOOTH EDGES WAS TOO COMFORTABLE

A SQUARE SHAPE WITH HARD EDGES SOLVED THE PROBLEM

"Luke," I sez, "I've solved her." That's what comes of bein' a specialist, gentlemen.

'Twarn't long after I built that twin job for the school house, and then after that the biggest plant up to date—an eight holer. Elmer Ridgway was down and looked it over. And he came to me one day and sez: "Lem, I seen that eight hole job you done down there at the Corners, and it sure is a dandy; and figgerin' as how I'm goin' to build on the old Robinson property, I thought I'd ask you to kind of estimate on a job for me."

"You come to the right man, Elmer," I sez. "I'll be out as soon as I get the roof on the two-seater I'm puttin' up for the Sheriff."

Couple of days later I drives out to Elmer's place, gettin' there about dinner time. I knocks a couple of times on the door and I see they got a lot of folks to dinner, so not wishin' to disturb 'em, I sneaks around to the side door and yells: "Hey, Elmer, here I am; where do you want that privy put?"

Elmer comes out and we get to talkin' about a good location. He was all fer puttin' her right alongside a jagged path runnin' by a big Northern Spy.

"I wouldn't do it, Elmer," I sez; "and I'll tell you why. In the first place, her bein' near a tree is bad. There ain't no sound in nature so disconcertin' as the sound of apples droppin' on th' roof. Then another thing, there's a crooked path runnin' by that tree and the soil there ain't adapted to absorbin' moisture. Durin' the rainy season she's likely to be slippery. Take your grand-pappy—goin' out there is about the only recreation he gets. He'll go out some rainy night with his nighties flappin' around his legs, and like as not when you come out in the mornin' you'll find him prone in the mud or maybe skidded off one of them curves and wound up in the corn crib. No, sir, I sez, put her in a straight line with the house and if it's all the same to you have her go past the woodpile. I'll tell you why.

"Take a woman, fer instance—out she goes. On the way she'll gather five sticks of wood, and the average woman will make four or five trips a day. There's twenty sticks in the wood box without any trouble. On the other hand, take a timid woman: if she sees any men folks around, she's too bashful to go direct out so she'll go to the woodpile, pick up the wood, go back to the house and watch her chance. The average timid woman—especially a new hired girl—I've knowed to make as many as ten trips to the woodpile before she goes in, regardless. On a good day you'll have you wood box filled by noon, and right there is a savin' of time.

"Now, about the diggin' of her. You can't be too careful about that," I sez; "dig her deep and dig her wide. It's a mighty sight better to have a little privy over a big hole than a big privy over a little hole. Another thing; when you dig her deep you've got 'er dug; and you ain't got that disconcertin' thought stealin' over you that sooner or later you'll have to dig again.

"And when it comes to construction," I sez, "I can give you joists or beams. Joists make a good job. Beams cost a bit more, but they're worth it. Beams, you might say, will last forever. 'Course I could give you joists, but take your Aunt Emmy: she ain't gettin' a mite lighter. Some day she might be out there when them joists give way and there she'd be—catched. Another thing you've got to figger on, Elmer," I sez, "is that Odd Fellows picnic in the fall. Them boys is goin' to get in there in four and sixes, singin' and drinkin' and the like, and I want to tell you there's nothin' breaks up an Odd Fellows picnic quicker than a diggin' party. Beams, I say, every time, and rest secure.

"And about her roof," I sez, "I can give you a lean-to type or a pitch roof. Pitch roofs cost a little more, but some of our best people has lean-tos. If it was fer myself, I'd have a lean-to and I'll tell you why.

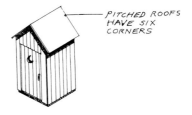

PITCHED ROOFS HAVE SIX CORNERS

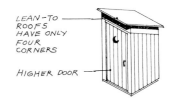

LEAN-TO ROOFS HAVE ONLY FOUR CORNERS

HIGHER DOOR

"A lean-to has two less corners fer the wasps to build their nests in; and on a hot August afternoon there ain't nothin' so discon-certin' as a lot of wasps buzzin' 'round while you're settin' doin' a little readin', figgerin', or thinkin'. Another thing," I sez, "a lean-to gives you a high door. Take that son of yours, shootin' up like a weed: don't any of him seem to be turnin' under. If he was tryin' to get under a pitch roof door he'd crack his head every time. Take a lean-to, Elmer; they ain't stylish, but they're practical.

"Now, about her furnishin's. I can give you a nail or hook for the catalogue, and besides, a box for cobs. You take your pa, for instance: he's of the old school and naturally he'd prefer the box; so put 'em both in, Elmer. Won't cost you a bit more for the box and keeps peace in the family. You can't teach an old dog new tricks," I sez.

"And as long as we're on furnishin's, I'll tell you about a technical point that was put to me the other day. The question was this: 'What is the life, or how long will the average mail order catalogue last, in just the plain, ordinary eight family three holer?' It stumped me for a spell; but this bein' a reasonable question I checked up, and found that by placin' the catalogue in there, say in January—when you get your new one—you should be into the harness section by June; but, of course, that ain't through apple time, and not countin on too many city visitors, either.

"An'another thing—they've been puttin' so many of those stiff colored sheets in the catalogue here lately that it makes it hard to figger. Somethin' really ought to be done about this, and I've thought about takin' it up with Mr. Sears Roebuck hisself.

"As to the latch fer her, I can give you a spool and string, or a hook and eye. The cost of a spool and string is practically nothin' but they ain't positive in action. If somebody comes out and starts rattlin' the door, either the spool or the string is apt to give way, and there you are. But, with a hook and eye she's yours, you might say, for the whole afternoon, if you're so minded. Put on the hook and eye of the best quality 'cause there ain't nothin' that'll rack a man's nerves more than to be sittin' there ponderin', without a good, strong, substantial latch on the door." And he agreed with me.

"Now," I sez, "what about windows; some want'em, some don't. They ain't so popular as they used to be. If it was me, Elmer, I'd say no windows; and I'll tell you why. Take, fer instance, somebody comin' out—maybe they're just in a hurry or maybe they waited too long. If the door don't open right away and you won't answer'em, nine times out of ten they'll go 'round and 'round and look in the window, and you don't get the privacy you ought to.

"Now, about ventilators, or the designs I cut in the doors. I can give you stars, diamonds, or crescents—there ain't much choice—all give good service. A lot of people like stars, because they throw a ragged shadder. Others like crescents 'cause they're graceful and simple. Last year we was cuttin' a lot of stars; but this year people are kinda quietin' down and runnin' more to crescents. I do cut twinin' hearts now and then for young married couples; and bunches of grapes for the newly rich. These last two designs come under the head of novelties and I don't very often suggest'em, because it takes time and runs into money.

"I wouldn't take any snap judgment on her ventilators, Elmer," I sez, "because they've got a lot to do with the beauty of the structure. And don't over-do it, like Doc Turner did. He wanted stars and crescents both, against my better judgment, and now he's sorry. But it's too late; 'cause when I cut'em, they're cut." And, gentlemen, you can get mighty tired, sittin' day after day lookin' at a ventilator that ain't to you likin'.

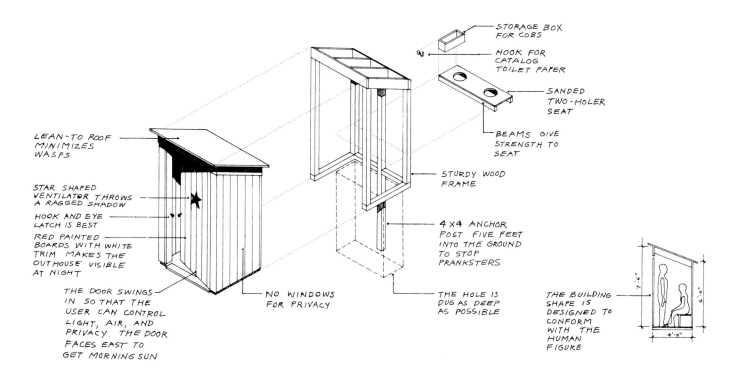

LEAN-TO ROOF MINIMIZES WASPS

STAR SHAPED VENTILATOR THROWS A RAGGED SHADOW

HOOK AND EYE LATCH IS BEST

RED PAINTED BOARDS WITH WHITE TRIM MAKES THE OUTHOUSE VISIBLE AT NIGHT

THE DOOR SWINGS IN SO THAT THE USER CAN CONTROL LIGHT, AIR, AND PRIVACY. THE DOOR FACES EAST TO GET MORNING SUN

NO WINDOWS FOR PRIVACY

STORAGE BOX FOR COBS

HOOK FOR CATALOG TOILET PAPER

SANDED TWO-HOLER SEAT

BEAMS GIVE STRENGTH TO SEAT

STURDY WOOD FRAME

4 X 4 ANCHOR POST FIVE FEET INTO THE GROUND TO STOP PRANKSTERS

THE HOLE IS DUG AS DEEP AS POSSIBLE

THE BUILDING SHAPE IS DESIGNED TO CONFORM WITH THE HUMAN FIGURE

7'-6"
6'-0"
4'-0"

"Now," I sez, "how do you want that door to swing? Openin' in or out?" He said he didn't know. So I sez it should open in. This is the way it works out: Place yourself in there. The door openin' in, say about forty-five degree. This gives you air and lets the sun beat in. Now, if you hear anybody comin', you can give it a quick shove with your foot and there you are. But if she swings out, where are you can't run the risk of havin' her open for air or sun, because if anyone comes, you can't get up off that seat, reach way around and grab'er without gettin' caught, now can you? He could see I was right.

So I built his door like all my doors, swingin' in, and, of course, facin' east, to get the full benefit of th' sun. And I tell you, gentlemen, there ain't nothin' more restful than to get out there in the mornin', comfortably seated, with th' door about three-fourths open. The old sun, beatin' in on you, sort of relaxes a body—makes you feel m-i-g-h-t-y, m-i-g-h-t-y r-e-s-t-f-u-l.

"Now," I sez, "about the paintin' of her. What color do you want'er, Elmer?" He said red. "Elmer," I sez, "I can paint her red, and red makes a beautiful job; or I can paint her a bright green, or any one of a half dozen other colors, and they're all mighty pretty; but it ain't practical to use a single solid color, and I'll tell you why. She's too durn hard to see at night. You need contrast—just like they use on them railroad crossin' bars—so you can see'em in the dark. If I was you, I'd paint her a bright red, with white trimmin's—just like your barn. Then she'll match up nice in the daytime, and you can spot'er easy at night, when you ain't got much time to go scoutin' around."

"There's a lot of fine points to puttin' up a first-class privy that the average man don't think about. It's no job for an amachoor, take my word on it. There's a whole lot more to it than you can see by just takin' a few squints at your nabor's. Why, one of the worst tragedies around here in years was because old man Clark's boys thought they knowed somethin' about this kind of work, and they didn't.

"Old man Clark—if he's a day he's ninety-seven—lives over there across the holler with his boys. Asked me to come over and estimate on their job. My price was too high; so they decided to do it themselves. And that's where the trouble begun.

"I was doin' a little paperhangin' at the time for that widder that lives down past the creamery. As I'd drive by I could see the boys a-workin'. Of course, I didn't want to butt in, so used to just holler at'em on the way by and say, naborly like: 'Hey, boys, see you're doin' a little buildin'.' You see, I didn't want to act like I was buttin' in on their work; but I knowed all the time they was goin' to have trouble with that privy. And they did. From all outside appearance it was a regulation job, but not being experienced along this line, they didn't anchor her.

"You see, I put a four by four that runs from the top straight on down five foot into the ground. That's why you never see any of my jobs upset Hallowe'en night. They might pull'em out, but they'll never upset'em.

"Here's what happened: They didn't anchor theirs, and they painted it solid red—two bad mistakes.

"Hallowe'en night come along, darker than pitch. Old man Clark was out in there. Some of them devilish nabor boys was out for no good, and they upset'er with the old man in it.

"Of course, the old man got to callin' and his boys heard the noise. One of'em sez: 'What's the racket? Somebody must be at the chickens.' So they took the lantern, started out to the chicken shed. They didn't find anything wrong there, and they started back to the house. Then they heerd the dog bark, and one of his boys sez: 'Sounds like that barkin' is over towards the privy.' It bein' painted red, they couldn't see she was upset, so they started over there.

"In the meantime the old man had gotten so confused that he started to crawl out through the hole, yellin' for help all the time. The boys reckonized his voice and come runnin', but just as they got there he lost his holt and fell. After that they just called—didn't go near him. So you see what a tragedy that was; and they tell me he has been practically ostercized from society ever since."

Well, time passed, and I finally got Elmer's job done; and, gentlemen, everybody says that, next to my eight holer, it's the finest piece of construction work in the county.

Sometimes, when I get to feelin' blue and thinkin' I hitched my wagon to the wrong star, and maybe I should have took up chiropracty or vetenary, I just pack the little woman and the kids in the back of my car and start out, aimin' to fetch up at Elmer's place along about dusk.

When we gets to the top of the hill overlookin' his place, we stops. I slips the gear in mutual, and we just set there lookin' at the beautiful sight. There sits the privy on that knoll near the woodpile, painted red and white, mornin' glories growin' up over her and Mr. Sun bathin' her in a burst of yeller color as he drops back of them hills. You can hear the dog barkin' in the distance, bringin' the cows up fer milkin', and the slow squeak of Elmer's windmill pumpin' away day after day the same as me.

As I look at the beautiful picture of my work, I'm proud. I heaves a sigh of satisfaction, my eyes fill up and I sez to myself: "Folks are right when they say that next to my eight holer that's the finest piece of construction work I ever done. I know I done right in specializin'; I'm sittin' on top of the world; and I hope that boy of mine who is growin' up like a weed keeps up the good work when I'm gone."

With one last look as we pulls away, I slips my arm around the Missus and I sez, "Nora, Elmer don't have to worry, he's a boy that's got hisself a privy, a m-i-g-h-t-y, m-i-g-h-t-y, p-r-e-t-t-y p-r-i-v-y."

Thank you, gentlemen.

Appendix

Kitchens and Bathrooms

The most difficult part of constructing your own home is, of course, the plumbing and electrical work. If you are willing to empty a chemical toilet occasionally, foregoing the luxury of the flush, or take the time to light a candle or oil lamp, foregoing the luxury of the switch, then there are simple solutions. This Appendix is written to help you decide on the kitchen and bathroom that fits your budget and immediate needs. All the bathrooms and kitchens discussed are ones that can be fabricated by an inexperienced builder. They are based on fixtures and appliances found in the four camping and recreational vehicle (RV) and van equipment catalogs listed in the Bibliography.

If you need a standard bathroom and kitchen with running hot and cold water, waste lines, electric stove, and refrigerator, it is recommended that you contact a well digger, a plumber, an electrician, and especially a septic system installer to insure that your plans are possible.

Kitchens

The smallest kitchen in the book is illustrated on page 118. It consists of a small cast-iron woodburning stove, primarily used for heat; a plastic, portable outdoor camper sink; and a small insulated ice cooler. The kitchens shown on pages 124, 128, and 186 use these same fixtures except they substitute a propane camper stove for the woodburning heater. These kitchens have elaborate but easy-to-build water supply systems, usable only if a nearby water source, such as a spring, clear stream, friendly neighbor, or spigot on a public building, exists. The stove and icebox are purchased to fit your needs and budget. The amount of cabinet work varies with each design but is necessary: tiny spaces, especially kitchens, need tiny places for everything or messy chaos can quickly result.

Refrigeration

Companies such as Sears, Coleman, or Montgomery Ward make a wide variety of insulated iceboxes, often called coolers. A nearby supply of block ice (cubes are fine but they melt faster) is necessary along with the energy to haul it from its source to your home. These coolers work well in keeping perishable food in the 45–55 degree range but will not keep frozen foods, such as ice cream, very long.

The RV and van supply companies offer a few excellent small LP gas-operated refrigerators, some with freezers. They are much more expensive than the coolers but eliminate the problems with the ice.

Water Supply And Sink Systems

The simplest water supply system is the portable outdoor camper sink, a carrier of five gallons of water with an indented sink space and pump-action faucet. A gravity-feed system like those shown on pages 114 and 186 can easily be installed for washing dishes, hands, and faces. This system, if used frugally, with care, will need only about ten to twenty gallons of water per day for a family of three. One of the more interesting water supply systems is shown on page 82. It supplies hot water from a black solar-heated storage tank, operated by a manual pump/faucet. The system is made of parts ordered from an RV and van catalog.

Sinks can be made from a plastic bowl, as shown on page 186, or simply purchased at a hardware or home supply center. Drainpipes can be hooked up easily with off-the-shelf plastic plumbing parts. The drainpipe should lead to a dry well, a pit dug as deep as possible and filled with rocks to disperse the waste water into the soil.

Stoves

A wide variety of two-burner propane-fueled camper cooking stoves are available through camping supply stores or catalogs. These stoves are used in the kitchens illustrated on pages 124, 128, and 186. A more elaborate LP gas-fueled cookstove can be purchased through the RV and van suppliers. Small portable barbeques and outdoor grills are available through hardware stores.

Heating sources can vary widely, and one should be carefully chosen to fit your climate and dwelling type. Propane catalytic heaters are available through camping catalogs and are a safe choice. A more permanent system, one used on pages 88 and 118, is the woodburning stove. These stoves often can double for cooking functions and can be purchased through a stove dealer usually available through the Yellow Pages. Kerosene heaters, used in the ice fishing shanties shown beginning on page 92, can provide quick warmth. They can be purchased at home centers and fuel supply outlets. Henry Thoreau's fireplace (page 39) should not be forgotten, but perhaps it should be replaced with a metal Heatolator or Majestic fire box. These are much more efficient and inexpensive heating systems. Because of its low installation cost, electric heat, baseboard or units, should not be overlooked if you have electricity available.

Bathrooms

The bathrooms shown in this book vary widely in size and complexity. The simplest bathroom is one like Henry Thoreau's (page 38), an outhouse with summertime washing in Walden Pond and wintertime washing with a large water-filled bowl. Most of the bathrooms shown here, though, have chemical toilets, a gravity-feed water system, and a simple shower system. More complex bathrooms, such as the ones on pages 103 and 111, require that an experienced plumber hook them up to a pressurized water supply system and a gravity-operated waste disposal system.

Toilets

The standard outhouse, as described by Chic Sale in his story beginning on page 207, is used with many of the houses shown in this book, especially the older ones. A well-kept outhouse is odor free and can be pleasant. A very inexpensive alternative to the outhouse, one based on the famous U.S. Army slit trench, is shown at the right. This little movable structure has been in constant summertime operation for seventeen years at my wilderness home in Maine, and has never failed to impress even the most civilized person.

Most tiny houses shown use portable chemical toilets, a relatively new invention for serious campers and RV users. They carry their own water supply, are odorless, and have detachable waste-holding tanks that separate quickly to empty into any permanent toilet facility. The quality and expense of these type toilets varies widely. The best selection can be found in the RV and van catalogs.

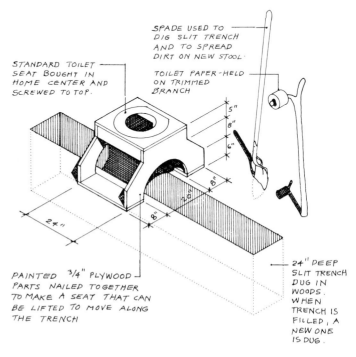

SPADE USED TO DIG SLIT TRENCH AND TO SPREAD DIRT ON NEW STOOL.

STANDARD TOILET SEAT BOUGHT IN HOME CENTER AND SCREWED TO TOP.

TOILET PAPER - HELD ON TRIMMED BRANCH

5"
8"
6"
8"
2'0"
8"

24"

PAINTED ³/4" PLYWOOD PARTS NAILED TOGETHER TO MAKE A SEAT THAT CAN BE LIFTED TO MOVE ALONG THE TRENCH

24" DEEP SLIT TRENCH DUG IN WOODS. WHEN TRENCH IS FILLED, A NEW ONE IS DUG.

Water Supply and Sink Systems

These systems are basically the same as those described under "Kitchens." In many houses, the same sink is used for personal washing as well as dish washing, for example, the Summer House kitchen and bathroom sink shown on page 114.

Showers

The simplest shower in the book is the black solar-heated plastic water bag with nozzle used on the rolling home on page 83. After it has been filled and warmed in the sun, it is hung on a tree or part of the house structure at shower height, for use. It is good for one quick shower and can be purchased from any camping goods store or by catalog. Most of the personal washing done in the tiny houses in this book is done with a large basin of hauled water and a sponge. Thomas Jefferson, said to be the inventor of the indoor privy, among other things, washed this way, and so did Henry Thoreau.

Showers can be fabricated in many ways. The most common method is the roof-mounted oil can, cut in half to catch rainwater, painted black to gain solar heat, and connected to a manually operated shower head. This method is used on many dune shacks (page 201) in the summer on Cape Cod. Another method is to transport water by plastic pipe (or bamboo sticks) from a stream at a high elevation to a place at a lower elevation where a person can stand up to have a stream of water flow from the last pipe and onto his or her head. The latter method would make a cold shower; the former, a warm one.

Bathrooms and kitchen designs are basically systems of gadgets that facilitate the flow of water, that heat and cook or refrigerate food. There are an infinite number of ways to perform these tasks. The system you design for your needs, site, and pocketbook will be, to a great extent, a product of your ingenuity and imagination.

Bibliography

Andersen, Robert, "A Vacation House You Can Build for Under $2,500 Complete." *Family Circle*, March 1972.

Beard, D.C. *Shelters, Shacks and Shanties*. New York: Scribner's, 1972.

Benson, Tedd, "Timber Frame Layout." *Fine Homebuilding* 16.

Blackburn, Graham, *Illustrated Housebuilding*. Woodstock, N.Y.: Overlook Press, 1974.

Burke, Bobbye, Otto Sperr, Hugh J. McCauley, and Trina Vaux, *Historic Rittenhouse*. Philadelphia: University of Pennsylvania Press, 1985.

Downing, A. J. *The Architecture of Country Houses*. New York: Dover Publications, 1969.

Frary, I. T. *Thomas Jefferson: Architect and Builder*. Richmond, Va.: Garrett and Massey, 1931.

Fraser, Henry, and Ronnie Hughes, *Historic Houses of Barbados*. Bridgetown, Barbados: Barbados National Trust, 1982.

Gaynor, Elizabeth, "Preserving our Pioneer Past." *Parade*, 12 August 1985.

Hendersen, Andrew, *The Family House in England*. London, England: Phoenix House, 1964.

Irwin, John Rice, *The Arnwine Cabin*. Norris, Tenn.: Museum of Appalachia Press, 1981.

Kauffman, Henry J. *The American Farmhouse*. New York: Hawthorn books, 1975.

Kimball, Fiske, *Domestic Architecture of the American Colonies and Early Republic*. New York: Dover Press, 1927.

Lancaster, Clay, *The Architecture of Historic Nantucket*. New York: McGraw-Hill, 1972.

Leitch, William C. *Hand Hewn*. San Francisco, Calif.: Chronical Books, 1976.

Lidz, Jane, *Rolling Homes: Handmade Houses on Wheels*. New York: A & W, 1979.

Maass, John, *The Victorian Home in America*. New York: Hawthorn Books, 1972.

McDole, Brad, and Chris Jerome, *Kit Houses by Mail*. New York: Grosset & Dunlap, 1979.

Miller, Fredrick M. *Still Philadelphia*. Philadelphia: Temple University Press, 1983.

Oak Bluffs Historical Commission, *A Centennial History of Cottage City*. Martha's Vineyard, Mass.: Oak Bluffs Historical Commission, 1978.

Poor, Alfred Easton, *Colonial Architecture of Cape Cod*. New York: Dover Publications, 1932.

San Francisco Chronical, October 1906.

Shelter Publications, *Shelter II*. Bolinas, Calif.: Shelter Publications, 1978.

Shumacher, E. F. *Small Is Beautiful*. New York: Harper & Row, 1973.

Shurtleff, Harold R. *The Log Cabin Myth*. Cambridge, Mass.: Harvard University Press, 1939.

Stiles, David, *Huts and Hideaways*. Chicago: Henry Regnery, 1977.

Stoehr, Eric C. *Bonanza Victorian*. Albuquerque, N.M.: University of New Mexico Press, 1975.

Thoreau, Henry David, *Journal of 9*, 9 April 1857.

Thoreau, Henry David, *Walden*. Salt Lake City, Utah: Gibbs M. Smith, 1981.

Vereins Kirche Archives Committee, *Fredericksburg: A Glimpse of the Past from Logs to Sunday Houses*. Fredericksburg, Texas: Gillespie County Historical Society and Commission, 1981.

Wagner, Willis H. *Modern Carpentry*. South Holland, Ill.: Goodheart Wilcox, 1969.

Walker, Lester R. *American Shelter*. Woodstock, N.Y.: Overlook Press, 1981.

Walker, Lester R. "Making a Living Cube for All Seasons." *Popular Science*, July 1974.

Weiss, Ellen, "The Wesleyan Grove Campground." *Architecture Plus*, November 1973.

Catalog, Coleman Outing Products

Catalog, Sears Roebuck Co.

Catalog, Montgomery Ward Co.

Catalog, Fredson RV and Van, 815 North Harbor Blvd., Santa Ana, Ca. 92703.

Acknowledgments

I am greatly indebted to the following people for their help in providing information for the book:

Thomas Jefferson's Honeymoon Cottage
Lucia S. Goodwin, Research Associate, Monticello

Frontier Cabin
John Rice Irwin, Director, Museum of Appalachia

Bandbox Townhouse
Janina Levy
Louise Axon

Henry Thoreau's Cabin
Anne R. McGrath, Curator, Thoreau Lyceum

Daniel Ricketson's Shanty
Anne R. McGrath, Curator, Thoreau Lyceum

Campground Cottage
Ellen Weiss
A. J. Goldwyn, Archivist, Dukes County Historical Society

Chattel House
Donald A. Wiles, Executive Director, Barbados National Trust

Sunday House
Louise Nixon, Chairman, Vereins Kirche Archives

Earthquake Refuge Shack
Jane Cryan, President and Founder, The Society for the Preservation and Appreciation of San Francisco Refugee Shacks
Jim Kanne, Images West

Pink House
Jean and Stuart Lamont
Borg's Ocean Front Motel
Mr. and Mrs. J. Williamson

Rolling Home
Jane Lidz

Mobile Tool House
Patrick Green

Portable Shelter Cart
Christopher Egan

Ice Fishing Shanty
John Baldwin
John Baldwin, Jr.
Tom's Bait and Tackle Shop, Lake Bomoseen, Vermont
John Lord
William Gorsky
Warren Furman

Cluster Shed
Timberpeg, Inc.
Richard Neroni
Jonathan Rose
James Dreisch

Backyard Retreat
Walpole Woodworkers, Inc.
Walter Carpenter
Kate Fraser

Bolt-Together House
Jeff Milstein

Summer House
Jeff Milstein

Cube House
Edmund L. Fuller

Tent House
Jeff Milstein

Canvas House
James Hadley

Picnic House
Michael Jantzen

Architect's Studio
David Minch

Guest House
Anthony Krauss

Poetry House
Carol Anthony

1950s Ranch House
David Minch

Autonomous House
Michael Jantzen

Fisherman's Shack
Christine Archer

Dining Building with Window/Chairs
Allan Wexler

Building for Picnicking
Allan Wexler

Little Building For Two Activities
Allan Wexler

Handmade House
Mary M. Carrabba

Recycled House
Graham Blackburn

Inside-Out House
David L. Bain

Dune Shack
Paul Pollets
Susan and Frank Richmond
Lawrence Schuster
Julie Schecter
Sunny Tasha
Hazel Hawthorne Werner

Photography Credits

The following people were immeasurably helpful and generous with their work:

Frontier Cabin
John Rice Irwin

Daniel Ricketson's Shanty
Thoreau Lyceum, Concord, Massachusetts

Campground Cottage
Dukes County Historical Society

Sunday House
Gillespie County Historical Society

Earthquake Refugee Shack
Jim Kanne, Images West
Charles Stern, San Francisco History Collectors Association
San Francisco Archives

Pink House
Stuart Lamont

Rolling Home
Jane Lidz

Mobile Tool House
Patrick Green

Portable Shelter Cart
Christopher Egan

Ice Fishing Shanty
Richard Dean

Cluster Shed
Timberpeg, Inc.

Backyard Retreat
Walpole Woodworkers, Inc.

Bolt-Together House
Jeff Milstein

Summer House
Jeff Milstein

Tent House
Jeff Milstein

Canvas House
James Hadley

Picnic House
Michael Jantzen

Poetry House
Reprinted by permission from *House Beautiful*, copyright © November 1985, The Hearst Corporation. All rights reserved. Photograph by William B. Seitz.

1950s Ranch House
David Minch

Autonomous House
Kristen Peterson

Dining Building With Window/Chairs
Allan Wexler

Building For Picnicking
Allan Wexler

Little Building For Two Activities
Allan Wexler

Handmade House
Mary M. Carrabba

Recycled House
Graham Blackburn

Inside-Out House
David L. Bain

All other photographs were taken by the author.

I also want to thank the Overlook Press for a job well done: In particular, Peter Mayer, who helped shape the tiny-house idea from the start; Deborah Baker and Kate Davis who provided such excellent editing work on the manuscript; and Janelle Berger and Irwin Rosen for their spirit and encouragement.

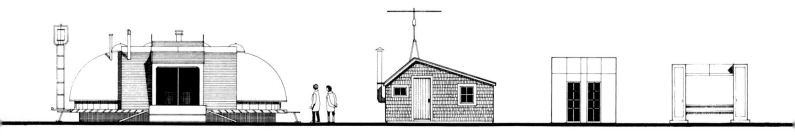